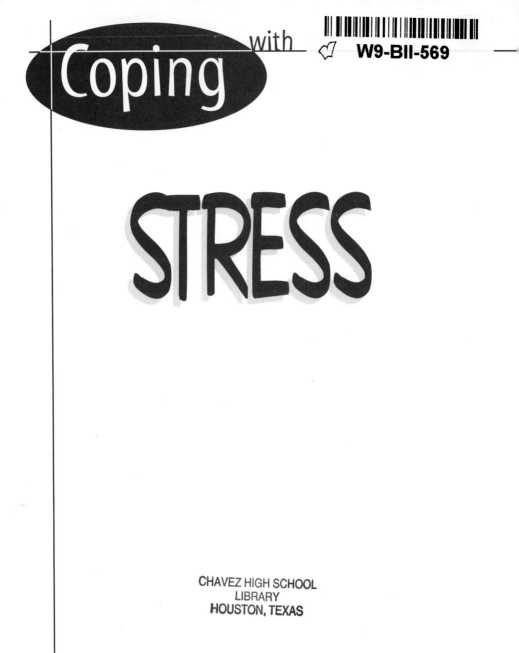

Coping with

STRESS

Gwen K. Packard

THE ROSEN PUBLISHING GROUP, INC. NEW YORK

Dedicated, with love, to Patricia Elsa Chang, M.D.

Published in 1997, 1999 by The Rosen Publishing Group, Inc.
29 East 21st Street, New York, NY 10010

Revised Edition 1999

Cover Photo by Olga Vega

Library of Congress Cataloging-in-Publication Data
Packard, Gwen K.
    Coping with stress / Gwen K. Packard. — rev ed.
        p.   cm. — (coping)
    Includes bibliographical references and index.
    Summary: A discussion of why teenagers may face stress and what
they can do about it, suggesting techniques for dealing with situations
such as school difficulties, relationships, and natural disasters.
    ISBN 0-8239-3042-4
    1. Stress in adolescence—Juvenile literature. 2. Stress management for
teenagers—Juvenile literature. [(Stress Psychology)] 1. Title. II. Series.
    BF724.3S86P33 1997
    155.9'042—dc21
                                                    96-52137
                                                       CIP
                                                        AC

Manufactured in the United States of America

About the Author

Gwen K. Packard has a Bachelor of Science in Education from Northwestern University and a Master of Arts in Library Science from Rosary College. She is a member of the American Library Association, Society of Children's Book Writers and Illustrators, Children's Reading Round Table of Chicago, and Off Campus Writers Workshop.

As a freelance writer, Ms. Packard is interested in parenting issues, education, and health care. She is the author of two other books for young adults, *Coping in an Interfaith Family* and *Coping When a Parent Goes Back to Work,* both published by The Rosen Publishing Group.

Acknowledgements

Many thanks to the following people who were generous with their time and knowledge: Ginny Anderson and June Penner, LINKS Youth Health Services; Craig Delamore, WBBM Newsradio, Chicago; Jeanne Felcan, American Red Cross, Mid-America Chapter; Jim Gorski, LCSW; Jane Gaitskill, MSW; Mike Hoffman, social worker, Naperville, Illinois, Police Department; Pamela Holtzman, Cancer Wellness Center; Samuel Huff, high school guidance counselor; Myrna Lopez, Big Brothers and Big Sisters of Metropolitan Chicago; Nancy Love, Charter Hospital; Greg Newman, M.S.; Dana Vance and her eighth-grade class; Charla Waxman, Linden Oaks Hospital.

A special thank you to Don Packard for information, inspiration, and patience.

I also want to thank the many teens who shared their experiences and opinions with me. Their names have been changed to protect their privacy.

Contents

Part 1

What Is Stress?

Identifying Stress

Spring has finally arrived. The snow has melted into rivers, and the bright green buds on the trees grow larger every day. Pedro has heard that spring is supposed to be the season of rebirth. If so, how come he wishes he could just curl up and die?

Through the closed curtains of his bedroom, Pedro can hear kids shooting baskets. The noise reminds him of his old friends, his old school, and his old neighborhood.

At his old school, he was a popular guy. Here, he does not have any friends at all. And who knows how long it will take him to fit in? The guys at Pedro's new school snub him, and the girls always seem to be giggling behind his back.

Pedro lies back on his bed and covers his head with a pillow.

Why couldn't his mother's boss have given the job of vice president to somebody else? Why did his mother have to uproot him in the middle of his most important year of high school and drag their family to another city? She never even asked him what he thought of the move.

Ever since they moved, Pedro has felt very angry with his mother. Even though he knows she feels a lot of pressure due to her new job, sometimes he feels like telling her off. But he doesn't.

3

Instead, he gets these strange pains in his stomach. The same ones he gets when he walks to school. Sometimes—like on Friday afternoons when Pedro feels like a loser because he has no weekend plans—the pains get very sharp.

To top it off, today he got back the results of a major chemistry test. At his old school, chemistry was Pedro's best subject. He had even planned on majoring in chemistry at college. He was shocked when he saw the D on last week's test. How depressing, especially since he had studied so much that he ended up with a splitting headache.

Response to Change

The headaches, stomach pains, anger, and depression that Pedro has been experiencing are all symptoms of stress. They are caused by the difficulties he has been dealing with in his new surroundings.

Stress is often a response to life changes and the need to adjust to those changes. While many changes are positive, such as going on vacation or getting a new job, some changes are negative, such as an illness of a parent. Any type of change or disruption in your life—whether it's mental, emotional, or physical—can cause stress. This is especially true if these changes seem to be out of your control.

Stress can make you feel frightened, angry, or even sick. If you feel your problems are too much for you to cope with, or if you feel unable to manage your daily life and unable to enjoy it, you are suffering from stress.

You also might be under stress if you have one or several of the following symptoms: headaches, backaches, stomachaches, dizziness, rapid heartbeat, depression, anxiety, anger, forgetfulness, or the inability to make decisions. Excessive smoking, drinking, or drug use may also be caused by stress.

As a teenager, you are encountering many changes in your life. You are developing physically, which can be exciting, frightening, and annoying at the same time. Your mental and emotional outlook is maturing as you take on new responsibilities and strive for more independence. Your relationships with your friends, family, and the outside world are shifting too.

The physical alterations that you and all teenagers experience can be stressful both physically and mentally. You may not feel emotionally ready for the physical changes that are taking place. You are trying to discover who you are and where you belong in the world. You want to be accepted by your friends and although many of the changes in your life are positive, they are all coming at once. You may be graduating from high school and going to work or to college, moving to a new town or city, or starting a new relationship. Or perhaps your friends are dating, and you are feeling anxious because you are not. These are all changes that require new thinking, learning, and adapting. All that can create stress.

Today's teens are exposed to a host of problems that teens in past generations were not confronted by. These range from gang violence, crime, drugs, and AIDS and other STDs to high divorce rates, alternate non-nuclear families, and increasingly complex career choices.

You are probably faced with events that you have never encountered before, and you may be reluctant to discuss your feelings with those who have more experience: your parents, teachers, or other adults. Some teens, like Pedro, may not even realize that they are under stress. They just know that something is wrong.

Symptoms of Stress

Before you can cope with stress, you need to recognize its symptoms.

"I know I'm stressed when I yell at everyone," says thirteen-year-old James. "If one more person asks me to do something, I'm going to lose it."

"When I'm under a lot of pressure, I get depressed. I just want everyone to leave me alone," says James's friend Rae. "That's not easy when you have three younger sisters."

"I feel like throwing things," says Steve. "One time I threw my mom's best china serving plate on the floor and broke it. I had more stress than ever after that."

"Until my junior year in high school, I was doing well, and I never had any problems taking tests," says Nancy. "Then I started thinking seriously about what college I would attend, and my parents began to put pressure on me to get better grades. I tried to study harder. Then, whenever I had a test, I couldn't sleep at night. The morning of the tests, I would break out in hives. It was awful."

"My parents finally recognized that stress was the root of all of my problems. We sat down to talk and tried to figure out how I could do my schoolwork without feeling so much pressure."

You may think of stress as an emotional or physiological reaction, or as something that is all in the mind. But stress is a lot more than mental activity. When you are under stress, both your mind and body are affected. In fact, stress can affect all aspects of the mind and body: physical, mental, emotional, and spiritual.

Physical and Nonphysical Responses to Stress

Throughout history, the body's response to stressful situations has been an important means of survival. For example, if a hunter encountered a wild animal, his choice of response was simple: he could use his weapons to try to kill the animal or use his legs to run and escape. Experts call this the "fight-or-flight" response. In today's world, the fight-or-flight response can still be useful. It can help us to escape a fire or survive a disaster.

To prepare the body for a fight-or-flight response, the adrenal glands release hormones, increasing the heart rate, breathing rate, and blood pressure. Muscles tense, the digestive system slows down, and eyesight is sharpened. The mind becomes alert and ready to respond.

Mario experienced the fight-or-flight response on the day he encountered three members of a rival gang, the same ones who had shot Mario's best friend the week before. "If I had been with my friends, or if I had had a better weapon with me, I would have stayed to fight, but I took off. I never ran so fast in my life. When I got home, my heart was pounding, my muscles were tightened up, and I threw up. I thought I was having a heart attack."

The stimuli that cause you to feel stress are called stressors. In response to these stressors, your body prepares for a fight-or-flight response. In today's world, this gut reaction is not always appropriate and effective.

For instance, if your parents tell you that they are getting a divorce, a fight-or-flight response is not going to help you deal with the anxiety and stress you will feel. However, your body will react the same way: increased heartbeat and breathing rate, sweaty palms, and tense muscles, no matter what the source of the stress is.

When the stressful problem is solved, your body can recover and restore the energy needed for the next response. If your life is hectic, you may be unable to give your body enough time to recover before encountering the next stressor. If the source of stress is an ongoing situation, you may feel continual tension, which could manifest itself as upset stomach or sleeplessness.

Stress can be very powerful. It can deprive you of your sense of control and security, and it can weaken your ability to cope with daily problems. Teenagers are not exempt from the physical symptoms of stress. When you are under stress, the systems of your body, including your immune system, do not function as efficiently as usual. Your body's resistance may decrease, and you will become more susceptible to illness and infection. Stress can cause migraine headaches, stomachaches, diarrhea, nausea, ulcers, back pain, skin disorders, dizziness, frequent colds, sleep disorders, and even high blood pressure, which may increase your risk of heart disease. If not treated, stress may lead to more serious symptoms, such as eating disorders, panic attacks, phobias, compulsive disorders, violent behavior, depression, or suicide.

Other possible side effects of stress are the inability to

concentrate; memory loss; flashes of anger; changes in eating patterns; increased use of alcohol, tobacco, and other substances; and prolonged feelings of anxiety or helplessness. Under stress, you don't think as clearly as usual, so you are more at risk of having an accident or injury while performing activities such as driving or using machinery.

Just as pain is an indication that something is wrong with your body, stress is an indication that some changes need to be made in your life. When you don't pay attention to stress or when you don't cope well with it, stress can have a negative effect on your life. When you are under a lot of stress, you may suffer from low self-esteem and have difficulty enjoying the positive things in your life. You may lose interest in school and stop paying attention in class, causing your grades to plummet; you may withdraw from participation in extracurricular activities and stop hanging out with your friends. You may exhibit odd or antisocial behavior that can't be tolerated in school, such as being argumentative or taking drugs. If you feel too much pressure to succeed, you may look for ways to fail in order to relieve that pressure.

A high school counselor has observed that under stress, some teens lose interest in their appearance. Many who are usually neat and physically fit suddenly start to dress in a sloppy manner and pay less attention to general hygiene.

The physical and emotional symptoms of stress are often similar, no matter what the source of stress. "It's really very odd, but I feel the same signs of stress before a big test as I do before an important football game," says sixteen-year-old Conner. "My heartbeat starts to race, my palms get sweaty, and my mouth gets dry. Sometimes just thinking about it freaks me out as much as the actual event."

Connor's reaction to stress is normal. The physical response is basically the same no matter what the cause. Your mental or emotional reactions to stress are less predictable because they are based on personal factors such as your lifestyle and attitude.

When you are under stress, you may feel that things are hopeless. You may feel anxiety, panic, or frustration. You may feel guilty, self-conscious, or restless. Your ability to make decisions may be reduced, and you may make more mistakes. For some teens, stress may even lead to extreme behavior such as vandalism, murder, suicide, or outrageous violent acts. After the two teenagers at Columbine High School in Littleton, Colorado, shot and killed twelve students and one teacher before killing themselves, there was speculation that their twisted behavior was how they chose to cope with the stressors in their lives. Whereas this is a very extreme example of outrageous behavior, other teens may withdraw, have low energy, and a lack of enthusiasm or hope. Any attention-getting behavior may indicate that a person is crying out for help in the only way that he or she knows how.

The death of a friend or close relative adds grief to the list of stress symptoms. You may feel physical pain, and you may want to die, too. You may feel that you can't do simple tasks. You may feel as if you have no strength or energy, or feel numb, sad, depressed, or guilty. Following a natural or human-made disaster such as a flood, hurricane, earthquake, or fire, you may suffer even more symptoms than you would from other sources of stress. If impending danger is apparent, you may feel anxiety, fear, flashbacks, nightmares, a lack of emotions, avoidance of responsibility, and the inability to concentrate before the disaster, as well as after. You also may feel dazed, easily startled, or like you want to withdraw.

"Until I moved to California, I had never thought about earthquakes," says fifteen-year-old Mishiko. "The first one I experienced registered 5.4 on the Richter scale. It broke Mom's dishes and left a big crack in the ceiling. After that, I started dreaming that an even bigger earthquake would occur. I couldn't sleep. I worried that the house would fall in on us during the night."

Stress can affect you spiritually, too. The spiritual symptoms of stress are different for everyone because each person has his or her own idea of spirituality. You may feel isolated from the higher power that you usually look to for comfort. You may believe that you must carry all of the weight of your problems on your own shoulders.

Who Gets Stress?

Different people respond in different ways to identical situations. Sula and Nick both had starring roles in the school play. During the first few weeks of rehearsal, Nick was enjoying himself. Then suddenly, a week before opening night, he felt a lot of pressure.

What if he forgot his lines? What if he messed up the sword duel? What if he got a big pimple? It seemed to Nick as if the whole play was riding upon him. He stopped going out with his friends and spent all of his free time going over his lines. Butterflies fluttered in his stomach, he could barely keep down his food, and in the end, a big pimple really did appear on his chin.

Meanwhile, Sula's behavior was completely the opposite. Sula was shy, and initially she had doubted whether she could pull off a starring role. However, as dress rehearsals approached, Sula felt increasingly confident. She surprised herself by making friends with the rest of the cast and going out with them every night after rehearsal. In the end, Sula had never had so much fun.

Despite their different attitudes, when the curtain finally went up, both Nick and Sula gave outstanding performances.

Everyone experiences stress sometimes, but people may react differently to the same stressor. If you know someone who never seems to be under stress, it may be because, in his or her opinion, a particular situation is not as stressful as *you* think it is. The physical response to stress—such as the release of hormones, increased heart rate, and muscle tension—is generally the same for everyone. However, the psychological reaction is usually not the same, due to differences in personality, viewpoint, and experience. People can, however, learn to be more resistant to stress.

People who are always angry are more likely to be affected by stress and develop stress-related illnesses. Optimistic people cope with stress better than those who have a pessimistic outlook on life. Psychologists classify some people as type A personalities. These people are often under stress. They are competitive and ambitious, but at the same time, they may have low self-esteem and constantly feel that they need to prove themselves by accomplishing more and more.

An assignment deadline can cause stress for one person and be a challenge and motivating factor for another. Some people view stressors as challenges rather than obstacles. These people probably have a positive attitude, and they are able to work out satisfactory alternatives to problems. They probably feel as though they are in control of events. Some people can find good even in a situation they don't like, such as a job.

If you have ever had a bad day, when everything seems to go wrong, you may notice that some of the things causing you stress on that day did not bother you in the past. How you view a stressor has an effect on your ability to cope. You can't always change a stressor or get rid of it, but you can change your perception of the stressor and your reaction to it.

Why Cope with Stress?

No one can be completely free of stress, so it is important to learn how to cope with it.

> ➯ **Coping with stress can reduce or eliminate the physical and emotional symptoms associated with stress.** Stress is more than just an emotional annoyance; if you do not reduce or eliminate your stressor, you may encounter serious physical problems. If a stressor is removed or reduced, your body can resist further damage and begin to repair whatever damage has already occurred. Otherwise your body may develop physical problems.
>
> If you have physical problems that are caused

13

by stress, you may spend a lot of time and money trying to treat the symptoms of these problems. Coping with the stress directly may eliminate many symptoms.

Besides physical problems, not coping with stress can also cause a decline in school or job performance and an increase in personal conflicts.

↪ **Coping with stress can prevent the development of more serious symptoms of stress.** If you are under constant stress, your body's natural defenses are weakened and you can become sick. If left unmanaged, stress can eventually lead to mental illness or complete physical exhaustion.

↪ **Coping with stress can build your self-esteem.** When you are under stress, you often feel a loss of control, and your self-esteem decreases. By coping with stress, you can gain some control over your response to stress even if you can't completely control the cause of stress. In taking action, you gain confidence and boost your self-esteem by demonstrating to yourself that you are not helpless.

↪ **Coping with stress is an important tool for living successfully.** As a teenager, you confront stressful situations just as adults do. Now is the time to learn how to cope with stress and to learn skills that you will use as an adult.

PART II
The Causes of Stress

Stressors come from many different sources. What causes stress for you depends on your life at home, in your community, and at school, your activities and relationships, and your own personality. There are some stressful situations that you can control, modify, or even eliminate, while others are beyond your control.

Change, and adjusting to change, are major sources of stress. As a teenager, you are experiencing numerous changes in your life, and many at the same time. You are in a period of transition. You need to develop new skills to cope with each change.

Your body is developing physically, and you think and feel differently than you did when you were younger. These important physical changes mean that you have to develop a new self-image. This puts stress on the emotions as well as on the body.

You need to make decisions about school, work, and college. Events beyond your control can disrupt your routine. It is important for you, along with your parents, friends, siblings, and teachers, to recognize when you are under stress.

In one survey, teens listed six categories that caused them the most stress: school, family problems, employment, relationships with girlfriends or boyfriends, friends, and college. Other sources of stress include violence, drinking, and unplanned pregnancy.

Stress can begin at home with conflicts between parents. At school, many teens feel stressed about doing homework, taking tests, and getting into college. These everyday worries can be compounded by stress from crises such as death, divorce, and natural disasters.

Teachers, parents, family members, and peers can be sources of stress. Stress can be caused by events and it can come from the way you treat your body. For instance, poor sleeping or eating habits or the use of caffeine, nicotine, or alcohol can cause stress. Stress can come from the way you think: Do you jump to conclusions or exaggerate problems? Are you too critical? Do you feel guilty?

Many of the stressors in your life cannot be avoided. However, even simply recognizing that stressors exist will enable you to better cope with them. At times you may feel as if you will not survive the many stressors in your life. But by developing your coping skills, you are well on your way to a healthier and happier lifestyle.

Stress in Your Home

It was a chilly winter morning and Angus and Nappy, both sixteen, were playing one-on-one hockey in Angus's icy driveway. "Take it easy," Angus warned as Napoleon slammed the puck against the garage door. "My mom is on the warpath. Ever since she lost her job, she gets on my case for the smallest things, like leaving the hall light on or not shoveling the walk. Having her around the house so much makes me constantly on edge."

"Well at least you know she's around," said Napoleon. "Ever since my folks split up, my mom's been going out with so many guys, I almost never see her. And some of them are real creeps. I worry that she'll get involved with a psycho that treats her worse than my dad did."

When a group of junior high school students were asked, "What is your greatest source of stress?" their immediate answer was, "parents." A group of older teens listed family as the second biggest source of stress, with school getting the highest vote.

One of the first things you may think of as a source of stress is conflict with parents or siblings. Even if you don't spend a lot of time at home—due to classes, school activities, an outside job, or being with friends—you are at home part of every day. You have to interact with your family, and this can be a source of stress.

"My biggest source of stress is my sister," says fifteen-year-old Ellis. "We're always fighting. I can't hang out at home because of her."

"My parents are my biggest source of stress, because of all the rules they want me to follow," says Wade, thirteen. "There's always something you have to do at home. If you don't do it right, you get criticized."

"My mom has set up a curfew. If you come in late, she gets worried. If you change your plans, sometimes you have to lie. That's stressful for me."

As a teenager, you are looking for more freedom and responsibility. This can cause conflicts that lead to stress. Often a conflict centers on a single issue, such as the use of the family car or staying out late at night. You want your parents to think you are mature. Yet at the same time, you want and need their support as you plan for the future.

Stress can be caused by parents putting excessive pressure on you to succeed. Your parents may expect you to follow certain standards of behavior that you and your friends do not agree with. You may feel guilty if you think that you are not living up to your parents' expectations.

"I have to keep trying to convince my mom that I'm not doing bad things," says fourteen-year-old Yusef. "She's always checking up on me, even when I stay after school for sports. When she compares me to my younger brother, we get into big arguments. That makes me angry."

On the other hand, your parents' behavior may embarrass you. "There are times when I want to pretend that my dad isn't my dad," says Adam, thirteen. "He does stupid things in public, or he yells at me. It really makes me nervous."

You may think that your parents are expecting you to

assume too much responsibility. You may not like helping out at home or taking care of younger brothers and sisters. This becomes a source of conflict and stress.

Of course, stress-related problems at home can go much deeper than arguing about who will take out the garbage. You may have to cope with money problems, divorce, the death or illness of a family member, single parenting, step-parenting, or substance abuse. If a parent loses a job, or starts working after a long period of unemployment, or if you have to move because of a parent's job, these are added stressors for your family.

Family Circumstances

Many family circumstances can add stress to your life. They may include the following.

If you are living with a single parent, he or she is under stress trying to handle obligations that are often taken care of by two parents. If your single parent is away from home a lot, there may not be someone with whom you can discuss your problems, which can cause you worry.

"My father ran out on us five years ago, and my mother works two jobs just to pay the rent," says seventeen-year-old Julita. "I raised my sisters myself. My mother wasn't there when I needed her, so I don't listen to her anymore."

If you are a foster child, you have to live with change and uncertainty. "I've been in different foster homes all my life," says seventeen-year-old Mel. "Just like my friends, I had the stress of staying in school and staying out of gangs. Adding to that was the stress of constantly adjusting to new foster homes, and new rules. I'm glad to say that I've learned to deal with stress. I'm going to graduate from high school, and I plan on attending college."

If you live in a blended family with a stepparent and stepsiblings, conflicts can arise because you must add the stress of accepting new family members, different expectations, and perhaps a different lifestyle.

If your parents are going through a divorce or separation, this is a major source of stress. "There was a lot of stress before my parents divorced, because of all the fighting," says Iris, fourteen. "Then there was the stress of the divorce itself. I had to deal with my own feelings and with my mom's feelings too. I can't understand why she was so upset about the divorce, since they never got along."

"Even though the divorce is now final, I still feel stress. When I know my parents are going to be at the same place, like parent's night at school, I feel sick to my stomach. I'm afraid they're going to fight in public."

"Before the divorce, when mom was fighting with dad she couldn't pay much attention to my problems. She still can't, because now she's a single parent and she has so many of her own problems to cope with."

If a close member of the family is seriously ill or has died, you are facing another powerful source of stress. You probably feel great sadness, fear, anger, and guilt. The rest of your family is experiencing the same emotions, so if your family does not work together to cope with this crisis, you may also feel abandoned and distant.

If there has been substance abuse (abuse of alcohol or drugs) by family members, or

If you have been the victim of sexual, emotional, or verbal abuse, you need to seek professional help, starting with a school counselor, a police officer, or a community social worker. (See chapter nine for more information on getting professional help.) Never feel like you must deal with these kinds of problems entirely on your own—even if other family members are telling you to keep things quiet.

When Your Parents Have Problems

Frequently, your parents' problems can create problems—and stress—for you, too. Your parents may be having trouble with work, marriage, or with their health. When parents are under stress, they can seem to be uncaring, extremely cranky, overprotective, or even angry and, in extreme cases, violent. He or she may exaggerate, generalize, or overreact to your problems.

Sixteen-year-old Collin explains his situation: "I know my da's under a lot of stress. His company is laying people off, and he doesn't know if he's next. Whenever I do something he doesn't like, Da says, 'You always do that,' even if I've never done it before. Once in a while, I'd like to talk to him, but he's so preoccupied that I can't."

Instead of helping their teenagers deal with stress, some parents create even more stress in the family. Many teens say that their parents do not spend much time with them and do not communicate well with them.

"My parents put a lot of pressure on me to do better in school," says sixteen-year-old Rajife. "It's frustrating."

Pressure to Perform

Are you trying out for a part in the school play, playing soccer in an important game next week, or hoping to get a good grade on the next math test? Are your parents telling you to improve your grades, get a job, and help out more at home? You may be feeling pressure, by both yourself and your parents, to do more and to do better. Many people in our society try to have it all. They want both personal and material success. But there is never enough time or money. The response is stress.

Your parents can be very demanding, but their high expectations—in moderation, along with support and encouragement—can have a positive effect. However, when expectations become too high, the result is stress.

If you think that too many pressures or high expectations are imposed either by your parent or by yourself, it may lead to anger, frustration, or unacceptable behavior. Anger adds to stress. You need to compromise, and that calls for communication. Conflicts at home are usually the result of misunderstanding and poor communication.

Your Self-Image

You may not be aware of it, but how you view yourself will influence how you view stress and how you cope with it. If you have low self-esteem or you fear failure, you are adding to your stress. When you are self-confident, you are better able to deal with stress, and you may not even think of certain situations as stressful. Most teens are concerned about being accepted. You are struggling with your desire to belong, while also wanting to be independent. You may even have considered joining a clique or gang to feel accepted by your peers. You are probably also concerned about your physical appearance. You are going though a period of physical change that may include growth spurts. It can be stressful when you don't like what you see in the mirror.

If you jump to conclusions, exaggerate problems, or make generalized statements about your behavior ("I'm *always* doing something wrong"), you will increase the amount of stress you feel.

You probably have your own goals and standards of achievement. If you do not reach those goals, you create stress for yourself. "I know I'm creating my own stress, but it's hard not to," says fifteen-year-old Felicia. "There are so many things I want to do aside from school, like getting a job and being a cheerleader. I know I'm not getting enough sleep, and I'm not eating right. When I'm tired or hungry, the smallest thing—for instance, losing my pen—can make me feel stressed out."

As you mature, you are faced with many changes in your life. You also need to make important decisions, such as whether you should go to college or get a job. Making important decisions can be stressful. You may feel stuck in your tracks, unable to do much else until you come to a conclusion, or you may rush to make a decision without giving it much thought and end up making an inappropriate decision. If you are reluctant to share your worries and concerns with your parents or teachers, try talking with your friends. You may not be aware of it, but keeping things bottled up inside you can be detrimental to your health. The more you repress, the more your problems get blown out of proportion, and you will be under enormous pressure. Talking can be very cathartic, so try to find someone—an older friend or relative, or a counselor—whom you are comfortable talking with.

In some cases, this may be easier said than done. It is possible that some people won't feel able to talk to friends or family members for fear of being judged. Sometimes, it can be easier to talk to someone who isn't involved in your day-to-day life. Part III of this book will direct you to other places to go for help.

Stress at School

"When I was younger, I used to like school," admits four-teen-year-old Lu. "But now it seems as if I spend all my time doing homework, writing essays, and studying for exams. I feel as though I don't have a life at all. Sometimes, it's as if I'm suffocating, but if I complain to my parents, they just say I'm lucky to be getting an education."

"I know what you mean," agrees sixteen-year-old Marvin. "I feel as if I never have enough time to finish all of my homework and assignments. To make things worse, my dad, who's a journalist, really pushed me to get involved in the school paper. At the beginning of the year, things were going smoothly, but now I'm falling behind. I would like to quit the paper, but there is nothing my dad hates more than a quitter."

"I was never interested in academic stuff," says seven-teen-year-old Vim. "I just want to get recruited by a good college basketball team, with a full paid scholarship. What with practices and games, who has time for home-work? Other teachers always understood how important basketball was in my life. But this year, I've got this English teacher putting pressure on me. She says if I don't shape up, she'll get me suspended from the team. If that happens, my future will be ruined. Basketball is my whole life."

Like Lu, Marvin and Vim, most teenagers find that school is the greatest cause of stress in their lives. Since it is there that teens spend most of their waking hours, it is not surprising that school produces a great variety of stressors both in and out of the classroom.

One of the biggest stressors comes from schoolwork. Schoolwork can often be overwhelming, whether it be too many assignments, homework that is too difficult, the stress of studying for and writing exams, or the pressure of getting good grades in order to be accepted by a good college or university. Further pressures may result from difficult relationships with parents, teachers, and principals.

There are other stressful factors at school that exist outside of the classroom. Extracurricular activities such as sports teams, dance teams, or participating in the school orchestra not only demand extra time and energy but can be sources of both physical and emotional stress.

Meanwhile, even day-to-day interaction with your peers can be a source of worries and problems. No matter what your age, everybody wants to be liked, respected, and accepted. But for teenagers, who are growing, changing, and experiencing many new things all at once, social life at school can often be complicated.

You want to fit in, but you don't want to have to drink or do drugs in order to be one of the gang. You want a girlfriend or a boyfriend, but you don't want to succumb to sexual pressure in order to keep your partner by your side.

Forging new relationships while trying to be accepted and not doing things that make you uncomfortable can create a great deal of stress.

Academic Performance

At school, the most frequent cause of stress is concern about academic performance. Some teenagers only care about getting grades that will allow them to pass or to graduate. Others feel pressure to get high grades that will help them get accepted into a good college or will increase their chances of succeeding in the profession of their choice.

"For a month before final exams none of my friends go out," says Luke, seventeen. "They all want As so that they will be on the honor roll when they graduate. They like to brag about how many hours they study without sleeping—sometimes twenty-four, sometimes forty-eight hours. Some of them take speed so that they can stay up all night and study. If I don't do the same thing, they think I'm stupid. If I do, I end up so exhausted that I can't think clearly when I sit down to write the exam."

Fifteen-year-old Samantha sympathizes. "I hate exams. No matter how much I study, once I'm in front of the exam paper and the clock starts ticking, I get so nervous. I just tense up and freeze. I never do as well as I think I should, and it really frustrates me."

"I used to totally dread giving oral presentations," says fourteen-year-old Maria. "Even though I knew the students in front of me were my friends, I would get so nervous beforehand that I would almost go to the bathroom in my pants. During my speech I could never look up, and I would say 'um' and 'like' a lot, even though I had spent hours rehearsing."

"My parents carefully supervise how much I study,"

says fourteen-year-old Ibrahim. "They think I don't work as hard as my older brother, who always got high marks. They compare me to him, which puts a lot of pressure on me. The only subject I do well in is English, which is good because I'd like to be a writer. But when I told this to my parents, they said I have to think about getting a real job."

"For me, it was the opposite," says Janice, fifteen. "My older sister was the pretty, popular one. She had lots of friends and boyfriends and was always going out to parties. I'm much less outgoing than she is and not as good-looking.

"To set myself apart from her, I tried to be perfect at school. If I got an A on an essay, I would argue with the teacher to give me an A-plus. If I got a 99% on a test, I would cry because it wasn't 100%. When my parents found out I was taking energy pills so that I could study all night, they got upset and made me see a counselor. At first I resisted, but after talking about my feelings I learned how to relax. I also made an effort to develop other interests outside of school."

"I only wish I had parents like yours," sighs thirteen-year-old Luigi. "When my dad was growing up in Italy, his father died of a stroke. Even though he was only fourteen, he had to drop out of school and get a job to help support the family. He never lets me forget how much he regrets not having a high school diploma. He's constantly on my case to pull my grades up so that I will do better than he did. If I bring home a less-than-perfect report card, he grounds me for weeks."

"I know how you feel," says sixteen-year-old LaRue. "My mom tells me that I am going to have to get grades that are good enough to win me a scholarship, because there is no way she is going to use up her savings to help me pay for medical school. With that kind of pressure on me, the smallest test becomes a huge deal."

School Activities

The pressure to obtain good grades is only one source of stress at school. Outside the classroom, many situations can also be stressful.

"This year I tried out for the football team to please my dad," says Liam, fourteen. "He's a football fanatic. I would have rather played badminton, but Dad says that's not a real sport. The problem is that I end up spending a lot of time on the bench. Before each game I get really nervous wondering if my dad will show up. When he does, and the coach doesn't let me play, my dad yells at him in front of all the other guys on the team. It's embarrassing. I've never been so miserable in all my life."

For Sharona, fifteen, it seems as if there are too many school activities and not enough time. "I've been playing the violin since I was five, so I can't stop now. And track is important to me because I need to do something physical. Then this year, all my friends decided to try out for the school play. I didn't want to be left out, so I auditioned too, and ended up with the lead! Now I'm completely overloaded and barely have time to do my homework. To make things worse, my parents are always complaining that I never help out around the house. They say that things will have to change, but I don't know what to do."

Sixteen-year-old Raul's father was injured in a construction accident, and his mother had to go back to work to support the family. Raul needed to get a part-time job as well. Every day after school he works in a restaurant. "I pay for my expenses myself," he explains. "The money I make is good, but the work is exhausting. By the time I get home and start my homework, it is usually 10 or 11 PM. Often I fall asleep at my desk and wake up in a panic because I didn't finish my assignment.

"Some of my teachers are understanding and give me extensions. But others are threatening to flunk me. As for a social life, forget it! I got kicked off the swim team for missing too many practices. And I'm lucky if I can go out with my friends once a week."

Aside from extracurricular activities, school social events can be nerve-wracking experiences. An end-of-year dance or a prom, for example, can provoke all sorts of pressures.

"Ever since I got my braces on, I feel ugly," says thirteen-year-old Meta. "I get very uptight just thinking about senior prom because I'm afraid that no one will dance with me unless I promise to keep my mouth shut. Otherwise, I'll blind them with all of the metal in my mouth!"

"My two best friends started talking about the June dance in March," says sixteen-year-old Lydia. "But that's because their boyfriends are taking them. My boyfriend broke up with me and now he is going out with another girl. For sure he is taking her to the dance. It seems as if everyone has a date except me, and I'd feel like a loser if I went alone. But I'd be miserable if I missed the dance. I feel like I'm in a no-win situation."

"I have a really big problem," admits Will, also sixteen. "I am gay and have just begun a really good relationship with a guy named Sam. All his friends know about us and they are cool, but I am afraid to tell any of *my* friends. Sam wants us to go to the prom as a couple. When I said no, and suggested going with two girls instead, he got upset and threatened to break up with me. I don't want to lose him, but the thought of my friends and parents finding out about us makes me want to die."

Major Changes

Change is a significant source of stress, and many changes take place while you are in school. "People are always telling you to set goals; that's supposed to help you cope with stress. My goals are constantly changing, creating more pressure," says sixteen-year-old Vince. "When I started ninth grade, I moved from a small school in my neighborhood to a huge school that I have to take two buses to get to. There seemed to be thousands of students, almost all of whom were older and bigger than me. All of a sudden I had difficult classes and more homework. My goal then was just to go through ninth grade.

"Well, I did manage to survive ninth grade, and now that I am in my third year of high school, I'm trying to make it to graduation. I also have to think about what I'm going to do after graduation. Should I go to college, or work, or what? If I choose college, I have to find one that will take me. If I decide to go to work, I'll have the stress of finding a job.

"Like I said, my goals keep changing. I have to make a

lot of decisions about those goals. Pressures are coming at me from all sides–from my parents, my teachers, my friends. The fact that I'm going to graduate is my greatest achievement. So many of my friends dropped out, and they pressured me to drop out too. That may have been the easiest solution. Of course my teachers kept trying to persuade me to stay in school. It caused a lot of stress along the way. I lost a lot of sleep. I stopped eating, then I started eating too much. Now, despite all the stress, I'm glad that I stayed in school. It makes me feel good that I survived."

Peer Pressure

In school and in your community, peer pressure creates a lot of stress. Your friends may encourage you to try alcohol or drugs or to engage in sexual activities that go against what your parents have taught you or what you yourself think. You may feel as if you are being pulled in many different directions at once. Who will you agree with? Is there a way to compromise? This is a source of stress.

Doing well in school and being accepted by the "in" group can be conflicting issues for some teenagers. That's what happened to Xavier, who was on the junior-varsity soccer team, was in the school play, and was one of the top students in his class. "I never talk grades with the guys. If I get an A, they'll call me a nerd," Xavier says.

For fourteen-year-old Roberto, good grades and security are linked. "I go to school far away," he says. "But if I don't keep my grades up, Mom will send me to school near home. No way. There are so many gangs at that school. That puts a lot of pressure on me to do well."

Negative Behavior

Teens who lack motivation and are not successful academically can also suffer from school stress. "I have a friend who wasn't doing well in school," says Nat. "She had so much pressure to get better grades, she thought about suicide. I told the school counselor, and I'm happy to say that she's fine now."

External Pressures

Some things that were once only the problems of adults have now come into the school and are sources of stress for teenagers. Many teens deal with the death of a classmate by murder, accident, or suicide. Students are carrying weapons into school. You, or others you know, may be cheating on tests. In many schools, drugs and alcohol are problems. Many of the stressors occurring in school these days used to be found only in the outside world, outside the home and school. But just as stress does not stop at the walls of your home, it doesn't stop at the walls of the school, either.

Stress from the Outside

Whereas for some teens, school itself is the biggest source of stress, for others real stress begins once they leave the school building. Tomas, a junior in high school, finds the walk to and from school much more stressful than actually being in school.

"After my dad took off, my mom moved us to a neighborhood that's pretty violent," he explains. "There's a lot of unemployment, a lot of drugs, and a lot of gangs. I know some of the guys in one gang. They used to be my friends before they dropped out of school and got mixed up with drugs.

"When I walk home from school, they razz me. They're always putting pressure on me to quit school and join their gang. They say that they'll protect me. But one friend I had who joined got shot last month by a rival gang. He was only fourteen. What kind of protection is that?"

Like Tomas, many teens have to deal with pressures from the outside world that are products of the environment in which they live. Whether they live in the middle of a big city, in a suburb, in a small town, or even in a rural area, teens are increasingly being confronted with complicated social issues such as gangs, drugs, and violence. Such problems can create a whole new series of stressors for teenagers.

Gangs are not only a big source of stress, but they also present true physical danger. Teens who live in neighbor-hoods with gangs have to deal not only with pressure to join a gang but also with the fear of being hurt or killed. Although gang warfare is rising, high school counselors say that it is still the worst in inner-city areas.

"I feel a lot of pressure to be in a gang," says Marco, six-teen. "In the end, it's easier to give in and join. Whether you do or you don't, you could end up dead either way."

Fifteen-year-old Frank agrees. "My older brother wasn't in a gang, but his friends were. They wouldn't let him hang out with them until he got a tattoo and a jacket like theirs. One time there was a drive-by shooting by rival gang members. My brother got a bullet through his spine and he's paralyzed. My mother says he's lucky."

Crimes and Violence

In many communities, the greatest source of stress is crime and violence and the fear of crime and violence.

Many teenagers have either been the victim of a crime or know someone who has been a victim. Often, both the attacker and the victim are teenagers. Crime and violence are daily occurrences in some communities. Teenagers who experience this daily stress are more susceptible to developing anxiety and fear.

Luanne, thirteen, says, "I'm afraid to walk to the next building because I might get shot by gang members."

People living in the midst of urban violence continually have to adjust to threats of death and violence while still trying to maintain their everyday existence. The stress is so great that some suffer from symptoms similar to those of survivors of war or natural disasters, such as fear, anxiety, irritability, depression, abdominal pain, chest pain, headaches, and sweating. Teens exposed to chronic stress may react by acting out or joining a gang.

Most teenagers, even those living in wealthy areas, say that they worry about crime. Fear of crime can be just as stressful as being the victim of a crime.

"So many bad things happen in my neighborhood, you become afraid of everything," says sixteen-year-old Wanda. "Just going to the corner store can be stressful. My heart beats fast, and my hands get sweaty even if there's no one around. Last week, I was going to the store to pick up a carton of milk for Mom when this weird-looking guy started to follow me. I crossed the street and ran home. It took an hour for my heart to slow down."

"I'm never sure how to act with the police," sixteen-year-old Marshall says. "Sometimes they treat you as if you're the criminal, when you haven't done anything. Other times they help you out. If too many kids get together, the police break them up. In our neighborhood, we can't even cruise anymore. That used to be our whole Saturday night. I know there are some police who treat kids disrespectfully, but I'm usually glad to see them."

Brian, fifteen, points out that violence is not the only source of stress for people living in the city. "It's too crowded. Our classrooms are full. Everyone is in a hurry. They'll knock you down if you get in the way," Brian says. "And don't forget about noise, dirt and pollution. Sometimes I feel like I'm living in a dungeon with no escape. I try to do what I can, like recycling and helping our church group clean up the neighborhood. But there are still so many things that I can't change."

Social Problems

Dealing with prejudice and racism can be a source of stress. Everyone shares the need to have friends and to be accepted, but you may have found yourself in a situation where you have been rejected—in either a subtle or obvious way—because of a mental or physical disability, your age, race, or other personal characteristics.

"It's stressful when people stereotype you," says fifteen-year-old Eric. "If they think you can't succeed because of your race or ethnic background. It gets me mad. I try to do my best at school and someone comes along and says, Oh, you must have cheated, you can't get high grades."

"I know what Eric means," says Nina, fourteen. Whenever I go into this clothing store near my home, someone follows me. I'm sure it's because I'm Hispanic.

"One day, I went into the store with some friends, and a salesperson started to follow us. Finally, I called her bluff. 'Do you think I'm stealing? Search me.' She didn't search me, but she never bothered me after that."

"Even some of my friends have racist views," Erica adds. "It makes me uncomfortable when they put down people behind their backs. They don't realize they're insulting me, too. It makes me wonder what they say behind *my* back."

Fifteen-year-old Hannah agrees. "When I'm with someone making anti-semitic remarks, I try not to let them know that I'm Jewish. That can be very stressful for me."

Nina laughs. "That's great for you, but if you are black or Hispanic, you can't hide it."

"People discriminate against me because I have long hair and earrings," says sixteen-year-old Mark.

"I'm discriminated against because I'm Arab," says Jamilah. "Especially after a terrorist attack, kids at school say my relatives did it. Well, I'm just as afraid of the terrorists as anyone. The discrimination doubles my stress."

Feeling Out of Control

Feeling as if you have no control over sources of stress becomes a cause of stress itself. In fact, those unable to cope with problems in their lives and in their community, such as drugs, violence, and pollution, may experience severe stress, which can lead to depression and even suicide.

You don't have to be a victim of a crime to experience stress. With actions beyond our control—like divorce, moving, unemployment, or a lack of feeling of permanence—we become insecure and feel stress. Simply witnessing something upsetting can be an emotional shock. Observing the death or illness of a friend or family member, seeing one parent abuse the other, or even watching upsetting news on television can cause stress. By watching television you see firsthand the results of war in distant places. This may cause you to overestimate the amount of violence in the world.

We are also getting cues from the media on how we are supposed to look and what we should be doing. There is pressure to achieve, look good, and be successful.

Fitting In

For you, the problems causing stress may not be as threatening to your well-being as those of other teens, but your feelings of stress are just as strong. Like most teens, you probably want to feel that you belong. You want to have friends. You want to feel good about yourself. When these things don't happen, you may feel angry, frustrated, or depressed; these are emotions that can lead to stress.

Thirteen-year-old Michael was always worried about friends. Who were his friends? Did they like him? What did they say about him behind his back?

Michael wanted to give a party, but he kept putting off sending the invitations because he was afraid no one would come.

"If you don't send those invitations soon, it will be too late. No one will be able to come," his mother warned.

Michael did send the invitations, and most of his friends said they would come. On the day of the party, Michael felt sick. He had a stomachache, and he couldn't eat breakfast. He hadn't slept all night. Now he was worried people wouldn't show up and that even if they did, they wouldn't have a good time.

"I'm sick," he told his mom. "I'd better call the party off."

"Don't be silly," his mother answered. "You're just nervous." Michael didn't call the party off. Except for one person, everyone who said they would come did come, and Michael thought they had a good time. "Yeah, the party was okay," he told a friend later. "But I'll never have another one; it was just too stressful."

Dating and Sexual Pressure

"My mom is always putting pressure on me about dating," says Beth, fourteen. "She tells me I'm too young to date. I'm not really dating. I just want to go out with my friends. Sometimes we just go to someone's house and hang out. Once in a while we like to ride around in one of the guys' cars. That's when mom really blows up."

"Mom probably worries that I'm going to have sex. On one hand, there's Mom saying don't have sex, and then my friends tease me because I'm still a virgin."

Sixteen-year-old Rolando says, "There's a lot of pressure to have sex in junior high. People tease you if you are a virgin. When you finally do *it*, the pressure is off."

Having a relationship with someone may be a new experience for you. And like any other new experience, you can become stressed out. You wonder how to act and what to do. What's appropriate? What's expected? How do your parents react to the situation? You may hear older friends or siblings talk about having sex on a date, drinking, or doing other things that you are not sure you want to do or are ready to do. Television, movies, and even popular music may make you think you need to be sexually active to be popular. This puts a lot of pressure on you. It's probably not a subject you want to discuss with others, especially your parents.

Whether or not to have sex can really cause a lot of stress, says Marci, fifteen. "You get pressure from your parents; you get pressure from your friends. Add to that the fear of getting AIDS or other diseases or getting pregnant. Some of my friends worry more about getting pregnant than getting AIDS. We all know that the best prevention is abstinence, but it's hard not to have sex when we see and hear so much about it in music, on television, and in the movies. And what about our hormones? Our bodies are telling us to have sex, too!"

At sixteen, Paco had always been shy around girls. One Saturday night, he went with some of his friends to a party in the neighborhood. Paco met Marla at the party, and he decided he wanted to go on a date with her. As Paco tried to work up the courage to ask Marla out, his stomach started churning, his heart beat faster, and he started to sweat. The whole time, Paco tried to appear calm and talk casually as if he had asked hundreds of girls out already.

Paco's stomach and heart didn't seem to calm down the whole week before his date with Marla. In fact, things got worse. Now Paco was worried about the date. Should he have sex with Marla? Would she expect it? Paco was getting mixed messages. He knew that his older brother and many of his friends had already had sex with their girlfriends—at least that's what they told him. On the other hand, his teachers and priest kept warning the kids that sex before marriage was not only immoral but might lead to some bad diseases, like AIDS, and of course, unwanted pregnancies.

The night before his date, Paco couldn't eat, even though his mother had fixed his favorite meal. "I don't understand you, Paco," his mother said. "You're getting all upset about this. It's only a date."

Paco couldn't explain anything to his mother. But he could talk to his older brother, J.J. It seemed as if he was always there for Paco. Even if J.J. did things that Paco did not agree with, he was great at listening. Sometimes just talking to J.J. was all that Paco needed to make up his own mind about a problem.

Stress about sex and dating is normal. It's also normal to be stressed out about the fact that you're not dating right now.

Trouble with Other Teens

Psychologists say that it is important for people to have some close personal relationships. In fact, a close relationship—whether it is with a friend or relative—is one way of coping with stress. However, your desire for a close friendship may conflict with striving to be independent. This can cause stress. You may have a conflict between wanting to be like your friends and wanting to be different. You want to be close to your friends, yet you are afraid of rejection.

As a teen, you are seeking acceptance by your friends, especially potential "special" friends that you are attracted to sexually. This can put pressure on you and can be quite stressful. In your effort to be accepted, your behavior may lead to even more serious stress-producing consequences, such as pregnancy or crime.

"Everyone wants to be accepted by others," says Zoe, sixteen. "That puts a lot of pressure on you and creates a lot of stress. Teens feel that they have to be just like the other kids. They're scared to be themselves. You may feel that if you are different, you won't be popular."

If some of your friends commit crimes, drink alcohol, use drugs, or engage in any other activity that *you* feel is wrong, you have some serious stress-producing problems to deal with. First, you must consider how your friends' behaviors influence your own behavior. Do you go along with them, even though you believe that what they are doing is wrong? Do you reject their behavior and perhaps risk losing their friendships? Or do you go even further than that and report their illegal behavior?

A police youth worker says that teens often get in trouble with the law because of peer pressure.

Fourteen-year-old Gail was confused about her relationship with Maria and Jackie. The three girls had been friends since they were in the seventh grade together. They were the first in their class to wear makeup and the first to go on dates instead of going out with a group or to a party. Maria and Jackie were friendly to Gail, and she liked that because she didn't have a lot of friends.

Often Gail got together after school with the other two girls. Gail didn't talk a lot, but she listened carefully. Gradually, through their conversation, Maria and Jackie revealed that they were shoplifting makeup, jewelry, and clothes from the mall. They invited Gail to join them on their next shopping spree. Gail tried to refuse politely. She did not want to get caught. It just wasn't worth it.

Gail began to feel more and more tension and stress when she was with Maria and Jackie. She wanted to continue to be their friend. She didn't want to be a snitch. She decided to keep their secret, even though she didn't like what they were doing.

After she found out about the shoplifting, Gail started to have headaches and stomachaches. Sometimes she couldn't concentrate on doing her homework or couldn't sleep because she was worried that someone would find out about her friends' stealing and that she would be blamed for not telling on them.

Gail decided to spend less time with the two girls, but she also noticed that they were making excuses not to include her in their plans as well. Eventually, Gail made friends with other girls who didn't want to associate with Maria and Jackie either.

Maybe you are not worried about your own behavior as much as you are concerned about your friends' behavior. You may sometimes feel embarrassed for a friend or embarrassed to be with that friend.

"I get annoyed with one of my friends," says fifteen-year-old Lance. "He's a real showoff. Sometimes he will do the stupidest things just to get attention. Then my other friends tell me I shouldn't hang out with him. When he gets in trouble with the teachers, they tell me to stay away from him or I'll get in trouble too.

"But I can't drop him as a friend. I've known him my whole life. We live in the same apartment building. He needs me to be his friend. If I dumped him, he would feel terrible. And I'd feel terrible too, worse than I do when others tease me about being his friend. It's a real problem for me."

Some teens join cliques or gangs to get the acceptance they don't find at home. Ben, fourteen, was lonely and wanted some friends. A few of the older boys in the high school, some of whom were in gangs, took advantage of Ben. They were friendly, making him feel like a part of the group. Then they started asking him to do bad things. Ben felt more stress than before because he had to decide whether to follow his conscience or do what the guys wanted. He was also afraid that they might hurt him if he refused to do what they wanted.

Sylvie didn't want to lose her boyfriend, so she went along with his pressure to have sex. Soon Sylvie was fearful that she might get pregnant or develop AIDS or another sexually transmitted disease. The stress from this worry caused Sylvie to have stomachaches. Sylvie thought that the stomachache meant she really was sick, so it only compounded the problem.

Because you are a maturing teen, you are expected to start taking control of your life. Others have high expectations of you. You are expected to take responsibility for your actions. You are now becoming a part of the community. You may be moving out of your parents' home, getting a job, or both. These changes can produce a lot of stress.

Stress on the Job

There are many ways your employment can cause you stress: if you need a job and have to look for one; if you're afraid of losing the job you already have; if your job takes up too much of your time; or if there is too much pressure put on you by your employer or your parents to succeed in your job.

Sixteen-year-old Sven says, "It's hard for a teen to get a decent job because of the economic situation. But some people just think we're being lazy when we complain."

If you have a job, you may experience a lot of stress there, too. You may feel some conflict with your supervisor or your coworkers. There may be a lot of competition or very high standards. You may also have a problem with your working conditions. If there is too much noise, if

45

your workplace is too small or too isolated, or if you are working with toxic materials, for example, your job can be very stressful.

"I really get worried when I'm at my job," says sixteen-year-old Hassan. "I work in a small factory, and I'm always reading about how dangerous chemicals and air pollution in a factory can make you sick."

"I help out at my dad's store after school," says Miguel, seventeen. "There have been a lot of store robberies lately. I wonder when it is going to happen to us. Sometimes I worry so much, I start to feel sick. Then I don't even want to work in the store anymore. But I know Dad needs the help. It would be worse if he had to work alone."

Change is taking place in your community and in the world. You are experiencing many changes firsthand. You must make decisions about finishing high school, going to college, or going to work, and even whether to move out of your parents' home and start out on your own. You are meeting rising expectations. There is a lot of pressure on you and other teens not just to get by but to achieve and be successful. You have to deal with these changes as well as cope with problems such as crime, racism, and personal relationships. The result is stress.

Critical Conditions:
Crises and Disasters

"I felt like the biggest idiot ever," fourteen-year-old Mila told her friend Julian. "It was right in the middle of the big science test. The classroom was completely silent. I felt a head rush coming on, and suddenly everything went black. I woke up a few minutes later on the floor. My head was in Mrs. Lebowski's lap and all the kids were crowded around me. I was so embarrassed, especially because I had wet my pants.

"Mrs. Lebowski was so nice to me. She took me to the nurse, who said I had probably fainted due to an accumulation of stress. After Mom had started chemotherapy treatment again, Dad had written a note to the principal explaining the situation. So Mrs. Lebowski and the nurse were both aware of what was going on at home with Mom in the hospital and me helping to take care of the younger kids.

"It was such a shock to us all when Mom went in for a checkup and the doctor said the cancer had returned and was spreading—especially after all we went through last year during Mom's first round of chemotherapy and her mastectomy. Dad especially is crushed. I have never seen him look so tired. As the oldest, I feel that all of the pressure is on me to look after my two little brothers. For them and for Dad, I really try to be brave, but secretly

I'm so afraid that Mom might not make it this time."

In a family, a crisis such as a serious accident or illness can produce big changes in everybody's lives, sometimes overnight. A crisis is a turning point in your life, the result of a radical change. Adapting and accepting the change, and then trying to deal with it, requires enormous effort. Such effort, as in Mila's case, usually results in a great deal of stress.

Crisis

Crises appear in a variety of forms and cause varying amounts of stress. What is known as a crisis is not always a bad situation. It may be a positive event in your life, such as recovering from an illness, graduating from school, or going on a vacation. A crisis may also arise from the loss of a relationship, such as a divorce or the death of a family member or friend. It can be a situation with lasting consequences, including a long illness, an accident, the loss of a job, or a natural disaster. Of course, there will be more stress resulting from your parents' divorce than from going on a vacation.

Others stress-producing crises include:

➥ Pregnancy or abortion

➥ A serious injury

➥ Moving

➥ Changing schools

➥ Breaking up with a boyfriend or girlfriend

48

➥ You or your parent getting a job or losing a job

➥ Starting or finishing school

➥ An encounter with police

➥ Witnessing or being a victim of a crime

➥ A parent leaving the household or remarrying

➥ Financial loss or gain

➥ A relative moving into your home

➥ Leaving home

➥ Going on a vacation

➥ Celebrating the holidays

➥ Any change in activities, habits, or lifestyle

Losing a Family Member

Probably one of the most stressful crises in a person's life is the death of a close relative, such as a parent or a brother or sister, or a close friend. The situation can cause a variety of emotions that result in stress. You may experience depression or great sadness at the loss. At the same time, you may feel angry with other members of your family, with the person who has died for abandoning you, or with God for taking that person. You also may feel guilty, asking yourself if in some way you may have caused the death or could have prevented it. You may feel helpless because you could not do anything to prevent the death. Feeling that you are not in control is often a source of stress.

In school and with your friends, you may feel singled out because of their sympathy for you following a death. You may feel left out because some people don't know how to relate to someone who has experienced a death in the family. If the death was the result of AIDS, murder, or suicide, it is possible that you may feel a certain amount of shame as well as sadness about the death. You may not want to discuss it with others, and your silence can add to your stress.

Loss of a Sibling

The death of a brother or sister can produce mixed feelings, depending on your relationship. Often a relationship with a brother or sister is a combination of affection, anger, and annoyance. Relationships among brothers and sisters differ greatly between families, depending on the difference in your ages, whether you are the same sex or not, and other factors. You and your brother or sister may not have been any closer than two unrelated people living in the same household. On the other hand, your sister or brother may have been a friend; someone you could talk to and learn from or teach; someone you competed with or argued with, yet who was an ally in disagreements with your parents. Either way, that brother or sister was a constant in your life, and losing him or her can be very stressful.

"My older brother Roland used to act as if I didn't exist,

except for when his friends came over. Then he'd make fun of me in front of them, to make them laugh," says Dolores, thirteen. "The time he made a crack about my breasts being small, I was so furious. I told him that I hated him and that I wished I was an only child.

"About a month later, Roland was hit by a drunk driver while he was crossing the street. He was in a coma for a week before he died. Somehow, deep inside, I felt it was all my fault—that God or some force had made my wish come true and taken my brother away. I felt this physical pain gnawing against my stomach. It was like having severe cramps. I couldn't eat and I couldn't sleep. I didn't dare talk to anyone. I was afraid that they'd discover what a monster I really was.

"Although my parents were devastated by Roland's death, they became concerned that I was looking thin and tired and was barely eating. Then one night, I woke up screaming with stomach pains. My parents took me to the emergency room at the hospital where the doctor said my pain was due to severe stress. The doctor recommended a therapist whom I began seeing twice a week. It really helped me deal with my feelings."

Losing a brother or sister if there are only two of you can be particularly complicated. Not only have you lost somebody who might have been a close friend and ally, but suddenly you become an only child. This can really change the balance within your family. Not only for you, but for your parents too.

On one hand, your parents might become very over-protective toward you. Their reaction to the death of your sibling might include a subconscious fear of losing you too.

On the other hand, your parents' grief might be so severe that, at first, they might not be able to help you deal with yours. You might feel as if you have not only lost your brother or sister, but your mother or father as well.

"When my younger brother Dylan died in a skiing accident, I thought I'd never get over it," says fifteen-year-old Donna. "It was as if a bomb exploded in my family. Everyone went flying in different directions and nobody seemed to be able to pick up the pieces and make our family close again.

"That was two years ago, and I still miss Dylan a lot. I guess I always will. Although it's easier now than it was at first. The first few months after he died I was so depressed I stopped caring about everything. I stopped seeing my friends and I couldn't concentrate on my schoolwork. Nothing seemed to matter.

"Luckily, I had a really great teacher who suggested I see a counselor. It helped so much to have somebody to talk to. Before, I could always talk to my parents about my problems, but after Dylan's accident they became total strangers. They were so wrapped up in their own grief, it was if I didn't exist.

"Then about a month later, my mom suddenly couldn't stop worrying about me. Each time I left the house, she would panic. Before Dylan's accident, my family used to go skiing all the time. But afterwards, my mom refused to let me go anywhere near a ski slope. I knew she was afraid of losing me too, but I needed to get on with my life.

"My dad's reaction to Dylan's death was completely different. He became this kind of zombie who just woke up, went to work, came home, and went to bed. He barely talked to Mom or me at all. My counselor said that Dad is taking longer to deal with his grief than Mom and me. But for a while, I felt like I'd lost not only Dylan, but Dad too."

Divorce

When your parents decide to separate or get a divorce, this situation may become a stressful crisis in your life. The divorce itself, as well as the problems that cause the divorce in the first place, can be sources of stress. You may respond to stress with a variety of symptoms.

After her parents' divorce, fourteen-year-old Sonia gained a lot of weight, and her grades went down. "I guess I stopped paying attention in class. Every time I started something, I'd think about the divorce, and I couldn't do any work," Sonia says. "Instead of doing my homework, I would go to the kitchen and eat a whole bag of potato chips or a carton of ice cream. It would make me feel better for a little while, but it didn't really change the stress I felt. It just made me fat."

"I guess at first I didn't realize how stressed I was about my parents' divorce," says Alan, fifteen. "I was depressed in school; I wasn't doing the work, and my grades were slipping. I got into a lot of arguments and even some fights, which I never did before. I kept trying to convince myself that Mom and Dad really weren't going to get a divorce; I told myself it was just another one of their fights, and they would get back together. Then I started getting terrible stomachaches."

The divorce of your parents can cause a variety of stressful situations. You may not see a parent as often as you would like. The parent you are living with may be working harder and may be more tired and have money worries. If your parent remarries, you have to adjust to your new stepparent and perhaps stepsisters and brothers.

You may feel as if you are caught in the middle, with each parent trying to get you on his or her side, trying to turn you against your other parent. There may be problems deciding custody, as there were for thirteen-year-old Andrew. "My parents fought about who would get custody of me and my sisters," Andrew says. "A judge finally had to tell them what to do, so now we're all with my mom. It was stressful during the custody hearing. I kept wishing Mom would give Dad another chance. Now it's still stressful because Mom and I argue a lot. I sometimes think that life would be easier if I lived with my dad. The truth is that it would be even more stressful, because the only time Dad pays attention to me, he is either yelling at me or criticizing me.

"My friend Nick lives with his mother during the school year and goes to live with his dad during the summer. That's tough too, because he has to leave his friends and even his brother all summer."

One of the most stressful factors in a divorce can be your guilty feeling that you caused the divorce, even if your parents tell you otherwise. "I thought my parents' divorce was my fault," says fourteen-year-old Martin.

If your parent is having emotional problems with the divorce, that can create added stress for you. Hannah, sixteen, felt that way. "My mother got so emotional about the divorce—one minute she was angry, the next she was depressed. She wasn't there for me when I was trying to sort out my own feelings, and I almost had to start taking care of her. I had to ask myself, 'What do I want Mom to do for me?' The answer was, I wanted her to be there to listen when I talked about my feelings. So I tried to listen to her, and eventually it helped both of us."

"Dad was usually on my side. Now that he's not living here anymore, I have to do everything Mom's way," says Tito, thirteen. "That makes my life even harder. As if I didn't have enough stress, Mom is getting married again. She is marrying a man with two kids, so I'm going to have a stepfather and two stepsisters."

"My parents are divorced but I get the most stress when they have to get together for my sake—like for parents' day at school or when I'm in a play," says sixteen-year-old Ingrid. "My heart starts to beat faster, and I get a dry mouth and a headache. I know it's not all stage fright; it's divorced parents fright!"

Pregnancy

Pregnancy entails a lot of changes for any woman and her family. However, for an unwed teenager, pregnancy can be an especially difficult and sometimes stressful situation. "A teen who finds out she is pregnant will have many mixed emotions, no matter how she deals with it," says a counselor who works with teenage girls. "With pregnancy come many changes, sometimes faced by the expectant mother alone. She may feel anxiety, fear, and shame."

The man who shares responsibility for the pregnancy may also feel significant stress. This situation has the potential to change his life as well as that of the woman.

He may feel pressure to get married, or he may not acknowledge his role in the situation. Whatever his feelings are, he will have to make decisions that affect his own life and his relationship with the woman.

The only sure method of preventing pregnancy is simply to avoid having a sexual relationship. But there is a lot of pressure on teens to have sex. Television, movies, and popular music often emphasize sex. Sometimes it seems like the kids who have sex are more popular. On one side, you may be getting pressure from friends and from your own body to have sex. On the other side, you probably feel pressure from your parents and other adults to abstain from sex. And you might not feel ready to have sex, either.

Job Status

Employment and unemployment are situations that can create big changes in your life and can cause stress. When you get a new job, or if you lose the job you have, you need to make adjustments in your life.

"For the first three months after I got an after-school job helping in the library, I had a constant sore throat," says sixteen-year-old Marisol. "Dad says it was stress because it was a new job. The same thing happened to Mom when she went to teach at a new school this year, and she has been teaching for ten years."

If a parent who has been working must stop because of a layoff, illness, or by choice, or if a parent goes back to work after not working for a long period of time, changes have to be made. The situation can cause stress for you as well as for your parent. Your parent's attitude may change, for the better or worse. You may have to take on responsibilities that you were never asked to do before, such as getting dinner ready or watching a younger sibling after school. Your parents may not have as much money.

"A few months ago, my dad's company merged with another company, and my dad was laid off. He was upset about it, really angry," says Eddie, fifteen. "When he was not just sitting and staring out the window, he was yelling at Mom, my sister, and me. Mom said he was under a lot of stress. Well, his stress was causing me stress. I was getting headaches. My teachers started to tell me I wasn't paying attention in class.

"We had to cut way back on our spending. I couldn't even go to the movies with my friends anymore. Then mom started to work more hours to help with everyday expenses. That was even more stressful for me. I felt as though I was living with two stressed-out adults, and there was no one to help me with my own anxiety. I didn't want to talk about it with my friends. Most of their dads were working, so I felt sort of weird because my dad was not working."

Disasters

Disasters include some of the most stressful events that can happen to a person and a community. They go beyond crises. A disaster may be considered a group of crises happening suddenly and all at once. Disasters may be natural or human-made and include floods, hurricanes, tornadoes, earthquakes, and fires. In today's world, disasters may also include chemical and toxic waste spills, airplane crashes, or terrorist attacks.

The immediate impact of a disaster may be death and injury, loss of home and other possessions, loss of community service, and relocation and separation of family. You may be separated from friends or family or have to live in a different area. Any of these factors can be stressors by themselves, but in a disaster they may all affect you at once.

It may take many months or even years to recover from the losses you suffer in a disaster. In the meantime, you may feel stress from emotions such as grief over the death of family and friends, guilt for surviving when others did not, fear, loss, helplessness, or abandonment. You or your family may even have to deal with the stress of going to court when charging someone with the responsibility of causing the disaster. News of a disaster is going to appear on television and in the newspapers and magazines. You may not be able to get away from reminders, which makes it more difficult to deal with your feelings and reduce your stress.

During and after a disastrous event, the fight-or-flight reaction that usually causes you stress can help you to survive the disaster and allow you to assist others. Sometimes, immediately following a disaster, if you and your family have survived and avoided death and destruction, there is a feeling of calm. Then disillusionment can set in, as you began to realize the extent of your losses. You may experience anger and grief and feel a loss of support, especially if you think a federal agency or insurance company that is supposed to help is not acting fast enough.

People who survive a disaster such as an earthquake may experience a variety of stress responses. Following a disaster, some people start talking about memories of traumatic situations that happened in the past. The event may stir up past feelings that have been held in for years. When you express your feelings about the disasters, you also may express your feelings about these past experiences.

"At first, I didn't want to talk to anyone about the hurricane," says sixteen-year-old Karina. "No one in our family was hurt, and I was glad about that. But our house was destroyed. Just thinking about it made me dizzy and sick to my stomach. I just wanted to crawl away somewhere and be by myself. There was a Red Cross mental health worker who finally convinced me that it would be better for me if I talked about the disaster.

"Once I started talking, I couldn't stop. All of a sudden, all these things that have bothered me in the past came spilling out, even the time the baby-sitter hurt me. These were things that I tried not to think about and had almost forgotten. It was hard to talk, because it brought back the bad feelings. But after talking I felt relieved, and it did help to reduce the stress I have felt for so long."

Life After a Disaster

As a teen, you are always trying to cope with a variety of stressful issues, such as problems in your family, in school, and in the community; and problems with friends, sexual relationships, and substance abuse. You may be concerned about economic issues such as money and housing. You and your family may already be dealing with divorce, illness, or death. These problems don't disappear when a disaster occurs but are sometimes made worse.

When you survive a disaster, stressful feelings come from the loss of normalcy. Many of the things you take for granted—such as the senior prom—cannot take place. What was once a normal situation becomes abnormal.

"After the tornado hit our neighborhood, it felt as if we were living on another planet, just like in *The Wizard of Oz*," says Paul, sixteen. "At least nobody was hurt, although we worried at first because we couldn't find everyone. They set up a shelter at the high school where we could eat and sleep until our house was safe to live in. I missed sleeping in my own bed and eating regular meals. We couldn't go to the mall or the movies because our car was wrecked.

"The longer we stayed at the shelter, the more depressed I got. When we could live in our house again, it was such a mess, I got even more depressed. I didn't want to do any of the things I used to like to do. If there was just a little wind or a loud noise, my heart would start to pound. Just a warning of a storm would make me stressed. Luckily my friends didn't tease me for acting like a baby. They seemed to understand how I felt even though the tornado hadn't hit their own neighborhood. My friends and the school counselor helped me get through this."

Post-Traumatic Stress Disorder

Some crises, such as a serious automobile accident or a fire, may cause an extreme stress response known as post-traumatic stress disorder. Symptoms include loss of sleep and nightmares; a mental replaying of the disaster, escape, and survival; and emotions such as guilt, anger, fear, and helplessness. This stress response is common following a natural or human-made disaster.

Expecting a Disaster

The waiting time between the warning of a disaster and the actual event, even if it never occurs, can be stressful. Angela, sixteen, says, "I live near Los Angeles. They keep telling us that someday there's going to be this massive earthquake that destroys California. Every time I feel a little rumble, I tense up. I'm afraid it's going to be the big one, and I'll never see my family again."

Whether you have been involved in a disaster or know someone who has, or if you have only seen disasters reported on the news, anxiety and fear of future disasters can cause stress. After the federal building in Oklahoma City was bombed in 1995, many people were afraid to go into any federal building.

"The Oklahoma bombing terrified me," says thirteen-year-old Bettina, who lives in another state. "My dad works in the federal building across the street from my school. How do I know that some crazy person isn't going to blow up his building too?"

Some people may deny the possibility of a disaster, especially a natural disaster, because they want to avoid the stress this might cause. They may ignore warnings and not take even simple precautions. However, preparing for a disaster or doing something to reduce the risk of a disaster gives you a sense of control and can help reduce stress.

"I live near a large forest, and there have been bad forest fires the last few summers," says Caitlin, fourteen. "I
started having nightmares about our house burning down.
I talked to my dad about it, and he calmed me down a lot.
He showed me where the smoke detector in our house is,
and together we installed a sprinkler system. We also
practiced a fire drill with the whole family. Now, even
though I can't stop a fire from happening, I feel better
about facing it if it happens."

In a crisis or disaster, you want to behave like an adult,
but you still feel insecurity and fear. You may not want to
show feelings such as guilt or grief because you think of
them as "childish" reactions. However, as a teen, your
reaction to a disaster is much the same as that of an adult.
Adults have the same feelings of helplessness and lack of
control. You go through the same anxiety and tension
leading to stress as adults do. Because you have less experience dealing with this type of situation, you may need
others to help you put the situation into perspective.

Part III
Coping with Stress

Stress can come from a variety of different sources. It is pretty much impossible to get through life without experiencing it at some point. Ultimately, life without stress would be extremely boring. Stress is a by-product of change, and change, even when difficult, is what makes life exciting and challenging.

Of course, some changes can create too much stress. If such stress isn't dealt with in a positive way, it can lead to serious physical and emotional problems.

To not let stressful situations get out of hand, it is important that you, your parents, and other adults in your life learn how to recognize the symptoms of stress and acknowledge that the stress you are experiencing constitutes a real problem. Many elements in your life can be the cause of your stress: your family; your friends; a relationship; school; a job; living in a violent environment; crises such as death, illness, divorce and pregnancy; and disasters such as fires or hurricanes.

What is essential is to find a way of dealing with your stress in a constructive manner that corresponds to your personality and your needs. A variety of techniques exist that can help you.

Using your mind, you can try to focus on the positive side of the changes you are going through. You can learn to rationalize your problems and, drawing from past experiences, you can learn to keep them in perspective. You can also put your body to work. Eating well, exercising, and learning relaxation techniques such as deep breathing and yoga can ease stress and make you feel better both physically and mentally.

It is essential not to withdraw from people around you. A big mistake is keeping your problems to yourself. Find a person or several people that you trust, respect, and feel comfortable talking to. Let them know how you feel and what you're going through, and don't be afraid to ask for their help. If you can't speak to family or friends, know that there are plenty of other adults—relatives, teachers, counselors, therapists, a family doctor, clergy members, hot lines, as well as support groups—all of whom can help you cope with your stress.

Even though they might make you feel better initially, drugs, tobacco, and alcohol are not useful options for combating stress. These substances might mask your problems, but they won't solve them. Often they only create new, more serious ones that will establish negative patterns of dealing with stressful situations in the future.

Although you are still young, you can use past experience as a guideline for coping. What has worked in the past and what has not? Accept that you can't solve every problem. Take into account your own physical and emotional limitations and have reasonable expectations.

Talking to Yourself: Using Your Mind to Cope with Stress

Daniel is a senior in high school and a very busy person. Besides attending classes (some of which are accelerated) he is codirector of the school musical and assistant manager of the junior varsity basketball team. On top of that, Daniel volunteers twice a week at the animal hospital because he wants to be a veterinarian.

"When I get home in the evening, my parents and my little brother have already had dinner," Daniel says. "I'm not usually hungry anyway. I'm exhausted, but that's the only time I have to do my homework. More and more often, I fall asleep over my homework. When I finally get into bed, I have trouble sleeping; and when I get up in the morning, I have a terrible headache. It's getting harder to do the things I have to do to get into a good college.

"Mom keeps telling me I'm under too much stress, and I should give up some of my activities before I really get sick. I don't think I can give anything up. I guess stress just goes with wanting to do a lot of different things."

Daniel is under a lot of pressure, and he is experiencing several signs of stress. Continuous stress—stress that continues for a long period of time—can lead to physical symptoms much more serious than a headache in the morning. When there is a lot of stress in your life, and it goes on for a while, you need to make some changes. But before you can make any changes to reduce your level of stress, you need to be aware that you do have stress and recognize the symptoms. Once you acknowledge that there is a problem, then you can start making the changes that will help you cope with stress.

If you have physical problems associated with stress, discuss them with a parent, a teacher, a counselor, or a doctor. Don't be tempted to treat just the symptom—such as taking something to relieve a headache—without also making some changes in your lifestyle to relieve the stress. Stress may show up as a physical symptom, but there is always an emotional factor as well. First, you need to identify the stressor: What is causing your stress? Then you need to consider your reaction to the stressor: Are you making the stressor more serious than it needs to be?

Sometimes, just one change in your life can make a big difference. Doing one thing differently is a start. If Daniel volunteers only one day a week or one day a month at the animal hospital, it might relieve a lot of pressure.

Taking some small action can help to alleviate some of your stress. Simply phoning a friend to talk is a step in the right direction. When you come up with a good plan of action, stick to it, but stay flexible enough to try other ideas.

Self-Talk

Talking to yourself and using your mind to cope with stress means setting goals, establishing priorities, getting organized, using problem-solving techniques, and taking action. You can develop a positive mental attitude, maintain your sense of humor, and stay in control while keeping everything in perspective. You can take responsibility for your own behavior and choose to act on your stress.

Be aware of your limitations, however. If a problem is beyond your control, you may need help from others. You might have to delay the resolution of a problem until you are able to handle it better. In that case, you need to accept the situation as it is, at least until a time when it can be resolved. Try to focus on what you *do* have control over. Do things in moderation; strive for excellence, not perfection. Forget about always winning.

When a situation makes you very angry or depressed, try to get away from it for a while so you can cool down and put it in perspective. You may need to set aside a problem until you can deal with it more effectively. Remember that a situation may be temporary and may be more manageable when you take a break from thinking about it.

Have a "one day at a time" and "one problem at a time" attitude. While you are in school, don't worry about those stressors that affect you at home or at work. When you are at home, let go of the things in other parts of your life that are bothering you. Thinking about everything at once can make the problems seem overwhelming, and you may think that you can't handle any of them. Don't dwell on past mistakes, and don't depend on tomorrow to be better. Plan for the future, but act for today.

The Power of Positive Thinking

Think positively. Be hopeful and realistically optimistic. Try to look at a stressful situation in a more positive way.

"When my boss yelled at me for doing something wrong, I was ready to quit," says Mitch, sixteen. "I thought, who needs the stupid job, anyway! There was just too much stress. Then I realized that I like the work, and I need the money. I know I can do a better job if I want to, so I'm going to try. I concentrated on doing things better by being more careful, coming in on time, and things like that. Well, it worked. The boss was happy, so there was less stress. I even got a raise."

When you're "talking to yourself," make up a positive or optimistic phrase that you can repeat to help reduce negative thinking, such as, "I can handle anything." At the end of the day, think of something new and good that happened during the day. Don't allow negative thoughts to overwhelm the positive. Stay away from negative people and people who resort to violence or use drugs to avoid their problems.

Sixteen-year-old Christie knows the value of positive thinking. "I had an argument with my friend, Alex, on a Friday afternoon. I'm afraid I said some things I shouldn't have, and I may have hurt her feelings. I felt guilty and depressed, but I couldn't talk to Alex all weekend. And the negative thoughts kept building up in my head; I was feeling queasy. I knew that I had to try to think of something positive or I would be stressed out. So I thought of all of the fun things we've done together.

"When I finally saw Alex on Monday, I had a positive attitude. I was able to smile and say 'hi' and really mean it. If I had let my stress build up, I may have been too angry, and who knows what I might have said. Instead, we worked things out, and we're still friends. I think it shows."

Allow Yourself to Have Emotions

Having a positive attitude is one way of approaching stress and coping with it. However, your positive attitude must reflect your feelings. Holding in feelings and just trying to look happy without working through the cause of your stress can only lead to more stress. Whatever you feel is okay, including anger; there are no right and wrong feelings. It's how you express your emotions, whether in a positive or destructive way, that is important.

Develop or maintain a sense of humor. Laughing is an emotional release. The person who said "Laughter is the best medicine" wasn't joking! When you feel stressed, smile and say something nice to someone else. You'll both feel better. Do something that makes you smile or laugh; but don't laugh or joke about your serious concerns. You should take them seriously.

Crying can also help to relieve some stress, and may even prevent a headache or other symptoms. Holding in your emotions slows down the process of coping with stress. Crying helps clear your mind so coping can begin.

Avoid the three kinds of negative thinking that one counselor calls "mind traps": exaggeration ("That's the worst thing I could have done."); generalization ("I always do the wrong thing."); and negative self-talk ("Boy, am I stupid."). Remember that everyone goes through stressful times and makes mistakes. Your situation is a normal part of the maturing process.

Setting Goals

Coping with stress should be goal-driven. You need to ask yourself: What are my goals? How can I reach my goals in a positive way? Will my decisions create more or less stress in my life?

Setting goals includes establishing priorities and keeping things in perspective. Some stressful situations are serious and may require professional counseling in order to be resolved. Other situations that may seem stressful for the moment are not threatening to your life or your lifestyle.

An important step in establishing goals is setting priorities. You can't do everything you want to do or have to do, and trying to do everything usually leads to a lot of stress. That is why you have to prioritize your activities; that is, put them in order of importance to you.

When you set priorities, you need to think about your values and your goals. There are some things you *must* do, such as go to school or to your job. There are things you *ought* to do: for instance, write Aunt Bea a thank-you note or clean your room. There also are things you *want* to do: join the track team or try out for the school play.

You can start by making a list of the tasks you have to do and want to do, with the most important ones first. Then do one task at a time, checking it off as it is completed. As you make your list, ask yourself, "Is this task necessary?"

You Can Say No
Give yourself permission to say *no* once in a while (but not all the time) to things you *ought* to do. When you feel pressured to do things you don't want to do, you are only wasting both physical and emotional energy.

You can cope with stress by saying no to something that will add to your stress. "I was honored when our senior class president asked me to be the chairman of the prom committee," says Jeff. "I had to think about it. I'm already involved in a lot of sports and activities in school, many hard classes, and even a part-time job. I finally said no, although that made me feel bad. I'm already stressed; adding one more thing would probably make me crazy."

When your stress is the result of a serious problem, such as the illness or death of a family member, you may have to think differently about the way you do things. You may need to postpone some decisions you are asked to make and some of the activities you are asked to take care of. This is the time when you have a right to say no to some requests.

Organizing Your Life

Get organized, and you've taken one big step on the way to reducing stress. What does it take to get organized? Try getting up earlier and giving yourself more time in the morning. Lay out your school clothes the night before. Make your lunch the night before. Have your books, sports equipment, and other school things by the door. You can avoid some of the mad scramble to find everything in the morning and start your day on a less stressful note. With your family, organize some tasks, such as meal planning and preparation, and other household chores, so that the family can work together. In this way, one person won't have the stress of doing everything.

Write everything down that you need to do and remember. Make lists. Make up a time schedule that includes those things you *have* to do, such as school, your job, homework, and household chores; also allow some time for the things you *want* to do, such as shopping or watching television.

While you are setting goals, listing priorities, and writing schedules, be sure to include time to do something you like that will allow you to tune out your worries for a while. That's what sixteen-year-old Vanessa did when she tried out for the soccer team. Vanessa is one of the top students in her high school class, taking advanced courses in English, math, and science. She has won awards for her English essays. She is also a member of the student council.

"Everyone thought I was crazy to try out for soccer when I had so much studying and so many responsibilities," Vanessa says. "I think they understand now that I needed soccer so that I could get away from all the pressures and stress. It really works. When I'm playing soccer, I don't worry about anything else. When I have to go back to studying I feel better about it. I also like being with people that I might not have met otherwise."

To help reduce stress, it is important to take time to do something you like, something that makes you feel comfortable, or something that makes you feel calm. You can choose from a variety of activities that will make you feel good and that don't involve a lot of planning, a lot of money, or a lot of thought.

An appropriate activity can be something as simple as eating a peanut butter and jelly sandwich, cleaning a closet, feeding the birds, or writing to a faraway friend. You can take a walk, read a mystery, take a bath, bake cookies, learn a new song, run a mile, start a collection, or volunteer to help someone who needs it. Do an activity on a regular basis that is calming for you. Occasionally you might do something with a parent that is calming for you both.

Sophia says, "When I feel stressed, I sit down and play the piano." Juan finds another outlet for his stress: "I like to go to a soccer game and scream at our opponents." Whatever the activity, it is important that you work it into your schedule.

When a member of your family is ill or has died, you may feel reluctant or guilty to do something that makes you feel better. However, even in this situation, it is important to do something you enjoy to relieve some of the stress you feel. You actually need to take a break from worry and grief.

Think About Your Problems

Besides planning work and recreation, you can set aside a special time in your schedule for worrying, too. This way, worrying won't interfere with the rest of your life, adding stress. Just thinking about your problems may lead you to a plan of action or a solution. Try not to worry about things that are beyond your control.

If the source of your stress is the illness or death of a family member or friend, set aside time to think about that person and your good memories of his or her life. Write about your feelings in a journal. In that person's memory, do something you enjoy. Share your memories with others.

Techniques for Problem Solving

Another way that "talking to yourself" can help you cope with stress is through the use of problem-solving techniques.

Sometimes stress comes from the feeling that you have no control over your problems. When you always rely on others to solve your problems, you lack control. However, when you work on solving your problems yourself, it gives you a sense that you can overcome difficulties. It gives you a feeling of self-worth and boosts self-esteem.

When you are under stress, or if you think a situation may begin to cause you stress, take a step back to understand the real problem and the best way to approach it. Size up the problem and consider the options to resolve it. Take time to think things through. Today is not the only day of your life. Think about alternatives, explore options, and look in new directions. You are putting yourself under pressure when you try to make immediate or impulsive decisions. Also, if you make a decision too quickly, you may realize later that you actually had other options that you did not take the time to consider.

Use a step-by-step plan to solve problems and reduce stress. Here's one approach.

➤ **Identify the problem.** What is the problem causing the stress? Focus on the true problem.

➤ **Explore solutions to the problem.** Look at a variety of options for solving the problem. Be realistic; keep in mind your goals and values. Prioritize your solutions based on how realistic and effective you think they may be.

➤ **Try one of the options** and see if it helps solve your problem. First, try the solution you think is best. If it doesn't work, try another.

You need a variety of coping options. Different situations call for different approaches, and you need to be able to choose your strategy. When trying to cope with a stressful situation, you may be able to change the stressor by modifying or eliminating it. On the other hand, you may have to change your own routine or lifestyle to avoid the situation. You may have to change your thinking: The situation might seem less stressful if you look at it with a more positive attitude.

Make Your Own Decisions

In order to avoid the stress that comes from peer pressure, you need to think for yourself. Decide if a situation is right for you without judging others. Your self-esteem will be boosted when you know that you can make your own decisions.

"Some of my friends were putting a lot of pressure on me to do drugs with them," says sixteen-year-old Guy. "It was causing me a lot of stress, until I decided that drugs just did not fit into my plans for the future. I made a decision, and I feel good about it. The stress is gone, at least in that part of my life."

Making your own decisions is an important step in the maturation process. As you learn to evaluate situations and to react according to how you feel is best, you are discovering how to rely on yourself. You are learning to develop an inner strength that will be with you for the rest of your life. You will learn how to live with both good and bad decisions, and this experience will help you make better choices in the future.

75

Looking to Religious Faith

Some teens will tell you that the best stress relief comes through religion and prayer. Some teens, such as fifteen-year-old Cassie, grew up in a religious home. "Religion has always been a part of my life," Cassie says. "I won't say that I have no stress, but I think that having faith sometimes helps. Getting ready for religious holidays can be really stressful, but you do get a secure feeling when you have all of those family traditions."

Other teens are discovering religion for the first time, either because there was no religion in the home or because they were not paying attention. "I started doing drugs when I was only thirteen," says Randy, who is now seventeen. "I think it was a response to stress. I was as low as you could get and still be breathing. My parents finally got me into a rehab program. That's when I learned that you don't have to carry the weight of the world all by yourself; there is a higher power, if you want to call it that, who can help. I'm not a very religious person, but I think religion has helped relieve a lot of my stress."

Mental Imaging

Mental imaging can help you respond positively to stress. If you have to give a speech, sing a solo in the choir, try out for cheerleading, or interview for a job, you probably anticipate that you will have some stress. Along with your preparation and rehearsal, try a "mental rehearsal," too. Visualize your performance, but also visualize the stress that you will feel and the best way to respond to that stress. A "mental rehearsal" can give you added confidence. It can positively affect your performance as well as your physical responses to stress. Mental images can help you relax.

Neal likes to think of lying on the beach.

"Believe it or not, I like to do math problems in my head when I want to relax," says Della. "When you're doing math, you can't worry about anything else; and anyway, if I make a mistake, who's going to know?"

Writing It Down

Writing can also help to reduce stress. When you write about the stressors in your life, you can clarify what is causing your stress, and you may come up with some solutions. Writing essays or poems helps to release tension. "Writing about my problems helps me feel better," says Carlos, fifteen.

You can keep a journal and write something every day, or write only occasionally. Have a special notebook and pen for your writing. Write about the causes of your stress, but write about the nice things in your life, too. Just writing down your feelings and your worries is a way to relieve stress. If a family member or friend is ill or has died, write about that person and your good memories. Through writing, you can clarify your problems in your own mind. If you like to draw or paint, you can illustrate your feelings that way, or create pictures to go with your writing.

Fourteen-year-old Tess used writing to help her cope with stress. "When my little sister, Liza, was injured in a car accident, she was in the hospital for several weeks. Then she came home in a body cast. Mom took care of her most of the time, but sometimes I had to stay home to help. I really had mixed-up feelings. I wanted to help my mother and be nice to my sister, but I also wanted to be with my friends and do things for myself. I didn't think it was fair. I got so upset about it that I started to feel sick.

"One day, when I was home and Liza was sleeping, I decided to write about my feelings. I wrote a little every day after that. Just writing down the things that I couldn't tell my mother or my friends helped me feel better. I even wrote a story to tell Liza. She liked it, and that made me feel better about her and about myself."

Compile lists, too. When you have a decision to make, make a pro and con list: jot down everything in favor of a particular action, and everything against it. This will help you weigh the decision. When you feel you are making a good decision, it gives you a sense of control. That is a positive way to reduce your feelings of stress.

Talking to Yourself

Talking to yourself helps to relieve stress by clarifying your problems in your own mind; helping you establish goals, set priorities, and get organized; and creating a positive attitude. Often you can take charge of your problems and your life and work to resolve your own issues. Taking charge of your life also means taking responsibility for your own emotions. You do have a choice. You can bring your emotions under control.

Talking to yourself is good, but you are not the only person you need to talk to. Teens often feel that they have to keep to themselves, but it is important to talk and to share with others: family members, friends, or counselors and other professionals.

Talk to yourself and others, take time to relax, and find the positive side of things. By keeping in touch with how you feel, you can give your mind what it needs to cope with a stressful situation.

Help Yourself: Using Your Body to Cope with Stress

"A couple of days before the big debate, I was so nervous that my stomach started acting up," says fifteen-year-old Merv. "I could barely eat for fear of not being able to keep my food down."

"Yesterday, I was furious when my boss yelled at me in front of everybody," says Bharati, seventeen. "The worst was that I couldn't talk back to him. Instead I got a splitting headache that lasted all night."

"Before the first game of the playoffs even began, I was sweating like a pig," says fourteen-year-old Robbie. "I was worried that I was coming down with some weird flu, but I guess it was just all of the pressure."

Physical Effects of Stress

The effects of stress show how your mind and your body work together. Stressful situations can lead to a variety of physical problems, including headaches, dizziness, stomachaches, rapid heartbeat, high blood pressure, tense muscles, anxiety, and skin disorders. If you treat your body appropriately, you can reduce the effects of stress on your body.

Because stress can lower your body's resistance to disease, you are more susceptible to illness when you have stress. That's why it is so important to take good care of yourself by eating right, getting enough sleep, and exercising. When your daily routine is disrupted following a crisis or disaster, you need to get back to normal as soon as possible.

Taking Care of Yourself

Eating right, getting exercise, and taking time to relax or have fun are always good ideas. These behaviors ensure that your body has what it needs to function properly. These practices can also help to reduce stress or even prevent it in the first place.

It may be possible to change your eating habits. If you like fast food or products with caffeine or sugar in them, such as soda, candy or desserts, you may not want to give them up too quickly. In fact, you may think that eating food like this reduces your stress because it makes you feel better. However, these foods contain stimulants, which can add more stress to an existing problem. Reducing such foods can help to reduce stress. Eating food to reduce stress can lead to overeating, which is a serious symptom of stress.

It is important to get a good night's sleep. If you have trouble sleeping, or are sleeping too much, this may be a sign of stress. "I've got to get at least six hours of sleep a night in order to function in school the next day," says Michelle, sixteen. "I try to finish my homework before I go to bed or in the morning; but even if I don't, I'm better off when I get enough sleep. Otherwise, I develop a headache or I feel dizzy. I have a bad attitude with my friends and even my teachers, and you know that's not good. Everything just goes from bad to worse when I don't get enough sleep."

The Value of Exercise

Besides eating right and getting enough sleep, try to include some exercise in your daily routine. Take part in individual sports, such as jogging, swimming, bike riding, or walking, or participate in team sports after school. Play basketball or baseball with friends in the neighborhood, or just throw around a Frisbee. Outdoor activities could also include mowing the lawn or gardening. You can do aerobics or yoga by yourself, with friends, or at your local park district or community center.

"My friends couldn't believe it when I went out for track, but it was the best thing I ever did," says Gina, seventeen. "I'm getting a lot of pressure from my teachers and my parents. I'd get so stressed, I couldn't sleep at night, and I would get headaches all the time.

"To fit in time for practice, I had to adjust my schedule, and that wasn't easy. Still, when I get out on the track and I'm running or jumping, I forget all about the work and the pressures and my parents, too. Even though I have less time for studying, I can work more efficiently and get more done. I feel better about it, too. I can really cope with the pressure now.

"My friend Monica says the same thing. She's in the gymnastics program after school, and it helps her cope with the pressures at home since her parents separated."

When you are under stress, your body reacts with a fight-or-flight response, which involves increasing your heart rate, breathing rate, blood pressure, and muscle tension. Physical exercise helps to use some of that energy and reduce the symptoms. Exercise is good for you mentally and emotionally, as well as physically. It can increase your self-confidence and self-esteem, help you feel in control, and improve your outlook on life. It can help you to relax and temporarily get your mind off other stressors in your life.

Start your exercise program slowly and build from there, especially if you have never exercised regularly before. In the beginning, plan noncompetitive activities that you can do by yourself or with friends, such as running or bike riding. This way you can work at your own pace, increasing your activity each day. Talk to your doctor about possible limitations and also suggestions for the best type of exercise for you. Plan your exercise time into your daily schedule, so fitting it in won't cause more stress.

Doing household chores, or any task or activity that you are committed to doing well and completing, can help reduce stress. These activities can keep you from getting bored (which can be stressful); they can take your mind off other stressful problems temporarily; and they can boost your self-esteem by giving you a sense of accomplishment. Your parents may also be appreciative of your efforts.

Breathing and Relaxation

When you engage in physical exercise, good breathing habits will increase your efficiency: You will use less energy while increasing the amount of exercise you do. Learning proper breathing techniques can help to reduce the symptoms of stress. If you are not breathing properly, less oxygen is going to your brain, and you can't function at full capacity. Deep, slow breathing is also one step in the relaxation process, another excellent method to help reduce stress and the symptoms of stress. There are a variety of relaxation methods that you can use, including progressive relaxation, breathing exercises, meditation, massage, and listening to quiet music. Just as stress has a usually negative effect on your body, relaxation can prompt positive physical changes. When you relax, your heartbeat and breathing may slow down, and there may even be a drop in blood pressure. Relaxation can help to reduce muscle tension.

The form of relaxing that you choose can be completely passive, such as simply lying down or sitting still and freeing your mind of distracting thoughts. Imagine something peaceful. "When I want to relax, I think about this picture I once saw in a magazine," says Risha, thirteen. "In the picture, someone was lying in a hammock, and the hammock was on a boat. It looked so relaxing. I know I'll never do anything like that; but when I want to relax, I think about how that must feel, and it helps."

With progressive relaxation, you progressively tense and then relax each area of the body. For example, you first tense and relax the muscles of the foot, then the calf, and then the thigh muscles, and so on. With this procedure, you concentrate on your body, learn to relax your muscles, and temporarily take your mind off your stress.

Relaxation may also come from just doing something you enjoy. Even when your stress is caused by a serious event, such as the illness of a family member, you need to occasionally take time out to do something that you like.

"When I try to relax by lying down or meditating, I feel even more anxious," says sixteen-year-old Afram. "I guess it makes me nervous to be doing nothing. But if I play jazz on the piano or listen to jazz, I really relax. I think jazz is the most relaxing music in the world."

Different people find different activities relaxing. In fact, what seems relaxing to one person may feel stressful to another. When a group was asked what they did to relax, answers included the following:

⮑ Take a walk   ⮑ Swim

⮑ Meditate   ⮑ Exercise

⮑ Read   ⮑ Pray

⮑ Play the piano   ⮑ Knit

⮑ Breathe deeply   ⮑ Imagine a happy time

⮑ Take a ten-minute nap

There are other techniques besides relaxation—including meditation, biofeedback, massage, and Restricted Environment Stimulus Therapy (R.E.S.T.)—that may reduce stress and the symptoms of stress. It is good to learn and use a combination of techniques.

Meditation

Through the use of meditation, you can reach a level of relaxation that is calming to your body and counters the negative effects of stress. To meditate, sit or lie down in a relaxed position, close your eyes, and concentrate on only one object or word, clearing your mind of other thoughts and distractions. Pay special attention to your breathing as you inhale and exhale. Your breathing and heart rate will slow down, and your blood pressure will be reduced.

Biofeedback

Biofeedback helps you understand and change the way stress affects your body. You select a bodily function which has been affected by stress that you would like to change or regulate, such as heart rate, blood pressure, skin temperature, or muscle tension. With the aid of electronic equipment, you monitor the function. You can learn to modify the function, and using mental and physical techniques such as imaging or proper breathing, you can reduce your pulse rate, blood pressure, tension headaches, or other stress symptoms.

"My muscles were getting so tense during gymnastics practice, I wasn't doing anything right," says Justin, fifteen. "Every time I made a mistake, it caused me more stress, so things kept getting worse. I think my gymnastics coach was afraid I might get hurt, so he suggested that I try biofeedback.

"The first time I tried biofeedback, I felt like I was in one of those old science fiction movies. They attached wires to my muscles and then to a machine that monitored the muscle tension. When my muscles were tense, the machine beeped; the more tension, the more beeping. Then, they taught me how to relax the muscles, so there was less beeping. After a while, I was able to recognize what muscles were tense and relax them even without the machine. Now I can relax before gymnastics practice and before a competition. I'm doing much better, and I have much less stress."

Other Activities for Reducing Stress

Massage can help to lower heart rate and blood pressure, improve circulation, and relax tense muscles. Massage will help you feel better psychologically. Through massage, you become more aware of your body and when it is experiencing the symptoms of stress, so that you can work to eliminate some of the sources of stress.

Restricted Environment Stimulus Therapy (R.E.S.T.) is a form of sensory deprivation. Participants float in a pool or lie down on a bed in a stimulus-free environment, with no light or sound. The air or water is the same temperature as the human body. Such an environment does reduce some of the effects of stress.

Taking care of a pet or a garden can often reduce your levels of stress and the symptoms of stress. "My dog, Ginger, is just a mutt we got at the Humane Society, but she's the best thing in my life right now," says fourteen-year-old Stacey. "When I come home from a stressful day at school, if a teacher has made me really angry, or I've had a fight with a friend, I know Ginger will be there to greet me. Ginger makes me feel so important, I can forget about my problems for a little while. When I need to talk to someone, Ginger is the one who is sure to listen; and she always seems to agree with me, too!"

"My garden is my stress reducer," says Quinn, thirteen, "Even though we live in the city where nothing seems to grow, I've got this big wooden tub out on the back porch filled with petunias and marigolds. The seeds are pretty inexpensive. I started the flowers from scratch inside the house. It makes me feel good that I have accomplished something worthwhile. Best of all, when I feel angry or frustrated, all I have to do is pull a couple of weeds, and I get relief!"

Take a break from your daily routine. Relax, have fun, and do something you like once in a while. Participate in a sport; paint a picture; listen to music; play an instrument; or do whatever makes you feel relaxed and happy.

Eighteen-year-old Linda likes to go to dance class after work. "Answering the phone all day, doing secretarial work, and putting things together for the boss, I sometimes feel like I'm running the whole office," Linda says. "My muscles tighten up and I'm sure my blood pressure goes up, too. So, when I get to dance class, all I have to think about is stretching out those muscles and moving to the music. It's a great stress fighter."

Charles, sixteen, likes photography. "My dad taught me photography. He was a professional photographer, at least until he got sick. I like to photograph people in the neighborhood. I know Dad likes to see the pictures, and I'm glad I have something to share with him.

"When Dad first got sick, I was afraid even to talk to him. It was very upsetting and stressful to me. I sometimes got sick to my stomach. Now that I'm sharing my interest with him, it's better. Photography also gives me time by myself to do something I like, and that helps with the stress. It makes me hopeful, too; maybe Dad will recover and we can work on photography together."

Volunteering

You can help yourself when you help others. Be a volunteer in your community—at the community center, with the park district, or at your local hospital, for example. Volunteer work has many advantages. It gives you a chance to think about something other than the events that are causing you stress; it builds your self-esteem because you are helping people in need and in your community; and it can keep you from getting bored. When you volunteer, you meet new and interesting people and make new friends. You can learn new things.

Volunteer work can have a more practical side, as it did for fifteen-year-old Jay. "I never thought much about plants and flowers, except when we had a biology assignment," Jay says. "Then the volunteer director at the community center told me that they needed people to plant flowers around the high school. I decided to sign up just to get away from home on the weekends. That's when my parents seem to do most of their fighting, and it's really causing me a lot of stress. I had to go to the plant nursery to pick up the plants. When I was there, I learned that there's a lot more to flowers than just something for Mom on Mother's Day.

"They are trying to grow healthy plants without using chemicals that are bad for the environment. I got so interested in the work, I started volunteering with the park district twice a month. I'm now planning to go into conservation or forestry after I finish high school. By the way, volunteering and doing something that interests me really did cut down on the amount of stress I feel. I don't get the bad headaches I used to get when I had to listen to Mom and Dad fight."

There are many ways to help yourself mentally and physically. Along with helping yourself, you may turn to others for help, too. Friends and family members, professional counselors, support groups and organizations are there to help when you are experiencing stress and the effects of stress. It's all right to ask for help.

Talking to Family and Friends

"When the hurricane warnings went up, I was scared," says fourteen-year-old Grant. "I didn't want anyone to know how I felt, even though it was giving me a headache and my heart was racing. Mom said we had to go to higher ground because of my younger brother and sister, so I agreed. I was glad the family could stay together, even though we weren't in our house.

"The Red Cross worker got some families together to talk. I didn't want to talk, even though she said it would be a good thing. I listened to the other families, and I realized that everyone felt pretty much like I did, even this kid from school who was older than me. Some of the families had gone through other bad hurricanes, and they survived. I learned that although the hurricane was bad, it wasn't the end of the world, and we would get back to normal some day.

"I finally said a few things about how I felt. I even suggested how we could entertain the younger kids so they wouldn't be so frightened, and everyone liked my idea. It's hard to believe, but I really did feel better after that. Like the Red Cross worker said, it was good to let my feelings out instead of bottling them up inside."

Expressing Emotions

When you are striving to cope with stress, two factors are important: You need warm and supportive relationships with family and friends, and you need to talk. However, when you are under stress, whether it's from a disaster or other problems, you may not want to talk to anyone or be with anyone. You need to recognize the benefits of talking to family and friends.

Just expressing feelings helps to reduce stress. Through talking, you learn that you are not alone, that you don't have to solve every problem by yourself. You discover that others have faced similar problems and survived. You can compare with others your responses to a stressful situation and know that you're not abnormal. Talking with others is also a positive action; you are reaching out to others rather than withdrawing.

Ideally, when you have stress, your home is the place where you can talk and where you find emotional support and encouragement. If you cannot talk to your parent or to an older sister or brother, try talking to a teacher, counselor, clergy person, neighbor, or another relative. Share your worries with someone you trust and respect.

Spend Time with Family

During times of stress, you should be able to rely on your family and friends for emotional support. In fact, the caring and understanding of others can help reduce stress. People who care about you can help bring a sense of comfort and trust into your life. Uncertainty, lack of control and change create stress in your life. Those who give you support can offer you predictable behavior and shared values. This can help reduce some of the stress or even prevent it in the first place.

When you seek the support of those who care for you, or when you are offering your support to others, you need to communicate. By talking to others, you share your feelings and you learn about the feelings of others. Don't assume you know what other people are thinking, and don't assume they know how you feel unless you tell them.

Take time to talk with your parents and other family members each day. Schedule a regular time for talking — such as before bed or after dinner—and stick to it as much as possible. Keep the television and other distractions off while you talk.

Besides talking with one of your parents (or instead of talking, if that is a problem) try doing some activity together. Plan something you both like, such as going to a movie and then eating out afterward. You can walk, ride bikes, or do some other physical exercise together. This may open the lines of communication and later you will be able to talk to your parent about more serious problems. Sharing an activity with your parent may help to reduce some of the stress you and your parent are feeling.

Talk to Someone You Trust

There are times when you may want to turn to an adult for information and support. However, you may feel, as many teenagers do, that you cannot talk to your parents. You may feel too embarrassed or think your parents will not listen or will criticize too quickly. Often a parent is unavailable, because he or she is working outside the home or simply does not want to communicate. You should be able to talk to someone outside the family. You can turn to other adults such as a teacher, school counselor, member of the clergy, a neighbor, adult friend, or the parent of a friend.

To sixteen-year-old Philip, it seemed as if he had never been able to talk to his father. Philip was having problems with some friends at school. The longer these problems went unresolved, the worse they got and the more stress Philip felt. Philip needed to discuss the situation with someone.

Every time Philip went to his friend Gary's house, Gary's dad was there. His dad had a home office. Occasionally, when Philip and Gary would go into the kitchen for a snack, Gary's dad would join them, and Philip would start talking to him. "I can't talk to my own dad like I can talk to yours," Philip told Gary.

"That's weird," Gary replied, "I think it's easier to talk to your dad." After a few conversations with Gary's dad, Philip was encouraged to try to talk to his own father about some of the problems that were causing him stress. Having people near you who care about you and who will listen to you is an important factor in reducing or avoiding stress. When you are under stress, it is a good idea to share your feelings with someone, whether those feelings are positive or negative. Just discussing with a parent, relative, friend, or neighbor how you feel can help to reduce the burden and let you know that you are not alone.

Just by talking, you can:

⮑ **Let off steam.** Before you can attack a problem, you need to calm down so you can think clearly.

➶ **Clarify problems.** Talking can sometimes help you focus on a problem. You can make choices and decisions. It can give you hope and ideas for action to help solve some of your problems.

➶ **Share ideas.** The person you are talking with may have some new ideas for you. He or she can listen to your thoughts and opinions and add to them or modify them. While talking, you may come up with some new solutions in your own mind.

➶ **Get encouragement.** You no longer have to feel as if you are dealing with your problems all by yourself. You are not alone.

➶ **Put things in perspective.** Another person's point of view and experience may help you see your problems, and the stress that goes with them, in a different light.

Seek Solutions

When you talk to a friend or with your family, discuss specific problems. Discuss alternatives to each problem and try to find realistic goals and solutions. Others should offer their support and not simply tell you what to do. Good communication should help you make your own decisions, not just give you advice.

Communicating in the right way can help you and your parents solve problems, negotiate, compromise, and settle differences. You want certain things from your parents, such as independence and moral and financial support. Your parents want things from you, such as appropriate behavior and success in school. Through communication and compromise, you and your parents can reduce the stress that these conflicting ideas might cause.

Discuss with your parents how you might handle a stressful situation. Discuss different solutions and possible results. If your parents' expectations and demands are the source of your stress, you can try making a contract with your parents for change. If you improve your behavior, your parents will reduce their demands or expectations of you. For example, you might agree: "I'll practice the piano for half an hour every day, and you'll stop asking me about it." Try to compromise and reach a balance, some middle ground, where neither you nor your parents feel you are compromising your standards.

You and your parents should establish some ground rules for your behavior at home. How will you handle your anger and your disagreements? Discuss the consequences of not following the rules. Know ahead of time what to expect if you don't keep up your end of the contract.

Communication Skills

Brush up on your communication skills. That includes not only expressing how you feel but also listening to the other person. Don't think up an answer while the other person is speaking; let her finish. Look for clues to her feelings in her behavior, tone of voice, and facial expression: Is she nervous, shy, angry, or sad? Express your own feelings about a situation without blaming others for the problem. Keep your sense of humor.

At the beginning of your discussion, try to get all the information you need by using active listening skills. Try to understand what the person is saying and thinking, not just from her words, but from her facial expressions and "body language." In your own words, repeat what the person has said so you know you understand correctly.

Don't drag up old arguments or old problems (some people call that "garbage dumping"). Remember the times you have resolved conflicts successfully. Don't be afraid to negotiate and compromise. Some issues can be negotiated, such as whether you need a haircut or whether you need to clean your room. Other issues cannot be negotiated, such as going to school.

Communication can reduce stress and also help avoid some stressful situations. You should speak up to express your feelings, but be sure to cool down first. Think about the problem and clarify your position; be specific. Talk about your own feelings. Don't blame someone else for the problem. Don't analyze someone else's feelings, ridicule him, or tell him how he should think or feel. Everyone is responsible for his or her own behavior. Be tolerant of other people's differences.

The following steps will help you and your parents solve problems and reduce stress:

> ⇒ **Discuss** one problem at a time. Be sure you and your parents are clear about the exact problem that you are discussing.

⮑ Everyone involved in the discussion should **offer ideas** on ways of handling the problem.

⮑ After all the ideas have been presented, each person may give his or her **opinion** of each one. **Eliminate** the options that have too many negatives or just won't work.

⮑ From the alternatives that are left, **choose** the one you will try; or, if necessary, create one.

⮑ **Try** out the chosen solution. Give it time.

⮑ **Analyze** whether the solution worked the way you expected it to. What was good about it and what was not? Then you can decide to continue with the solution as it is, modify it, or choose to try something different.

"Everybody tells you to discuss your problems with your parents. Well, we don't exactly discuss things in my house; it's more like an argument or a real fight, if you want to know the truth," says fourteen-year-old Leon. "At least my dad hasn't thrown me out of the house yet. My dad's strict rules are giving me a lot of stress. When he yells at me, it adds to the stress.

"Most of the time it's about my curfew. My dad wants me home even before the city curfew. That's not fair, because all my friends get to stay out at least until then. My dad always brings up the one night I came in late. That was a year ago, but he's still throwing it in my face, and usually just as I'm going out the door. The situation got so bad, I started to get stomachaches just thinking about it. I thought maybe I should just sneak out before Dad could yell at me, but that only made me feel worse.

"When I complained to my teacher, he said my dad and I should try discussing this problem when we're both calm, and not just as I'm going out. He said I might be able to negotiate something. I would never have believed my dad would do that, but he did. Maybe he was getting tired of yelling.

"When we discussed it, Dad listened to my reasons for wanting to be with my friends, and I listened to why he was worried about me being out late in our neighborhood, which isn't the safest in the world. We talked about ways to compromise, and we finally worked it out. Dad said I could slowly work up to the city curfew, as long as I always came in on time. He also said that the first time I came home late, my curfew would be put back even earlier than before. I agreed to that, and you can bet I haven't been late since!"

Pick a Good Time to Talk

Calm down before communicating. Don't talk over a problem when either you or your parents, or all of you, are already angry. You can't have a meaningful discussion when you feel so stressed that you are ready to explode. Don't just blurt out your complaint or criticism. Make an appointment for a later time, when you and your parents are ready to talk and listen. You might need to be by yourself for a while until you calm down.

Talking Leads to Understanding

Talking and listening help you and others understand each other's feelings. You can share and exchange feelings as

99

well as ideas for solving problems. When you share problems, you feel better knowing you are not alone.

If you think you are being asked to do too much at home—such as household chores and child care—and it is causing stress, you and your family need to communicate and negotiate. You can work together to reduce some of these tasks. Plan with your family how you can share some of your responsibilities at home, change them, or eliminate them altogether.

Of course, you can talk with people your age too. Talking to friends is probably what is most comfortable for you. Although another teen may not have the knowledge or experience of an adult, he or she can help, especially when the stressful situation involves another friend or a teenage brother or sister.

Coping with a Family Illness or Death

If a crisis such as a serious accident, illness or death of a family member, a divorce, or the sudden unemployment of a parent is causing you stress, you must deal with the problem as well as the stress it causes. Your parents may be hurting or grieving, but they can help you, too. You should be kept informed about the status of the ill or injured person or the cause of death. You should be included in events such as memorial services, and even help with some decisions. Know that it is all right to grieve or worry. It's okay for *anyone* to cry. Holding in these emotions and not expressing them can lead to serious physical and emotional symptoms of stress.

If your stress is the result of trying to cope with the serious illness or death of a parent, brother, sister, or friend, some special measures need to be followed. You will want to know what's going on, and you have a right to be told by your parents. Parents may be reluctant to tell you the truth because they are afraid it will frighten you. However, it can only add to your stress if you suspect that something is wrong but your parent denies it or gives you inadequate information. You will probably want to know the details of exactly what the problem is (for instance, if a parent is dying of cancer), how it will affect the person with the disease, how it will affect you, and what is going to happen in the future.

After you are given the right information about the illness affecting your parent or sibling, you may want to take part in his or her care, helping to reduce your own stress as well as bringing some happiness to the patient. At home (or in the hospital if regulations permit) you can read to the patient, decorate the room with pictures, or do something special that would bring a smile to the patient.

When Rosa's little sister, Carlita, was very ill following open-heart surgery, sixteen-year-old Rosa and her fourteen-year-old brother, Luis, were told all about the problem as well as Carlita's chances for recovery. Rosa was worried about Carlita, so worried that she couldn't sleep and seemed to have a constant headache. When Carlita was out of intensive care, the hospital allowed Rosa to come and read to Carlita. Rosa also brought pictures and made little ornaments to hang near Carlita's bed. Doing these things made Rosa feel better; her headache disappeared, and she was able to sleep at night. Rosa knew it made Carlita feel better, too, even though Carlita sometimes fell asleep before the end of the story.

Luis contributed in his own way by acting like a clown, making faces and bumping into things. Carlita laughed and called it "funny stuff."

When Carlita came home from the hospital, Rosa and Luis welcomed her. Now the family was faced with new stress because Carlita still required care at home. Once again, the family got together and talked, planned, and compromised. Carlita would receive the care she needed, and Rosa and Luis would still have time for school, activities, and getting together with friends.

With some illnesses or accidents, you realize that the family member will not recover. When a parent or brother or sister is dying, you need to make the most of your time left together. Even if you have never been close to this parent or sibling, doing things for him or her is more important than ever to them and for your own peace of mind.

A teen can do many things to help in a household when a family member is ill or dying. However, a teen should never be expected to take the role of a parent. Instead, try to arrange for another adult, such as a relative, neighbor or friend, to help with driving and chores, keeping the school informed, and communicating with people outside the family.

Following the death of a family member or close friend, it may take time before the family will be able to talk together. How long it takes to get to this point will differ with each member of the family. The family will need to talk, however, to share memories and feelings, to make decisions, or to plan a memorial service, event, or fund in memory of the family member who has died.

If death or illness affects your family, it is a time when you can ask others—such as a family friend, cousin, aunt or uncle, or neighbor—for assistance. When a family is grieving, people will offer to help, and it is all right to accept that offer. On the other hand, you may want to do something to help others, such as caring for a younger family member. Death or illness is out of your control, and that can cause stress. Helping others can help you feel more in control, which can help to reduce your stress.

Coping with Guilt

Guilt is another stressful emotion that you should work out by talking with others. You need to talk to an adult who understands your feelings, as fourteen-year-old Jack did. "When my little brother, Stu, got beat up by some punks while he was waiting for me to pick him up from school, I felt like it was all my fault," says Jack.

"I know that Stu gets out of school at 3:30 PM, so usually I'm there on time. But that day Shanice asked me to have a soda with her. I've always had a big crush on Shanice, so I couldn't refuse. By the time I showed up at Stu's school, it was 4:15 PM, and Stu was lying all bloody on the sidewalk. I felt so terrible. I couldn't eat or sleep. I even broke out in hives.

"I felt so guilty that I didn't want to talk to anybody about what had happened. I finally confessed to Father O'Leary at church, and that made me feel a bit better. He was understanding and said that I could talk to him any time I wanted. Just knowing I could confide in someone was a big relief."

A stressful situation that leaves many teens with feelings of guilt is the separation or divorce of their parents. It is not uncommon for teens to partially blame themselves when their parents split up. No matter how upsetting a time it is for everyone involved, it's important to keep the lines of communication open between you and your parents and to make sure you understand the real reasons for their separation or divorce. Also, don't feel embarrassed about opening up to friends and other adults who have gone through the same situation. Sharing experiences can help you feel less alone and give you other perspectives on how to cope with your problems.

"Right around the time my parents decided to get divorced, my friend Jan's parents divorced as well," says fifteen-year-old Masha. "Because we were both going through the same situation, we could identify with each other's problems. Helping one another through that stressful period cemented our friendship."

"Before my parents divorced, my dad was never around," says Pete, sixteen. "I think he was unhappy at home, but he stayed with my mom for the sake of me and my sister. I kind of sensed that, and it made me feel guilty. When they finally split up, my dad became a much happier person. Now, even though he no longer lives at home, we have a much closer relationship."

"My parents' breakup was really ugly. Neither one of them could stand to hear the other one's name mentioned," says Juliana, thirteen. "I'm just lucky my big sister was around. Although in the past we didn't always get along, she really helped explain things to me."

"When I was thirteen, I developed a very serious illness called Hodgkin's disease," says fifteen-year-old Brad. "I spent a lot of time in and out of the hospital. My mother quit her job to take care of me, and my dad had to take out a second mortgage to pay for medical expenses. My illness put a lot of strain on my parents. They ended up fighting a lot. Soon after I got better, they separated. Although they said it wasn't my fault, I felt guilty anyway. We went to family counseling together. The sessions made me realize that my parents' marriage had been in trouble long before I ever got sick."

"As if my dad abandoning us wasn't bad enough, my mom had to go back to work just to keep a roof over our heads," says fifteen-year-old Clark. "I went from having two parents to no parents, because it seemed like my mom was never around. It got lonely being at home, so I took to hanging out at the mall. I even started shoplifting. I guess I wanted attention. Well, one night, the cops brought me home and my mom made me talk to her. We sat down and set aside a specific time for the two of us to go to a movie, watch a football game, or just talk. Now, things are better."

Even if your parents are in the middle of a divorce, you should try to keep your life as normal as possible in order to reduce stress. The same is true following a disaster.

Dealing with a Disaster

Your family can work together as a unit to prepare for, go through, and recover from a disaster. Following a disaster, family ties may be strengthened as you discover that it is more important to preserve close relationships than material possessions. Talk with your family and friends about what has been lost. Talk with other families; share your feelings and your grief.

It is also important to talk with the mental health workers who will probably come to help during a disaster. Discuss the facts of the situation, but also discuss your fears and other feelings. Try to get back to normal as soon as possible, or at least carry out some of the tasks you normally do.

When you are going through a crisis or a disaster, you experience a great deal of stress. To relieve some of that stress, try to find something good in a bad situation. Sometimes a bad situation, such as a serious illness or a natural disaster, will pull a family together that was never close before. Many people who go through a tough time change their whole attitude about life and set new goals.

When you are under stress, you need to talk to others and you need to be with other people who are supportive and encouraging. However, if you think that talking with family and friends is not helping, you may need to go a step further and speak with a professional counselor or join a support group.

Talking to Counselors and Support Groups

It was two o'clock in the morning, and seventeen-year-old Sandra had been sitting on the edge of her bed for almost two hours. She should have been relieved now that exam week was over, but the stress of the past week had left her numb. Sandra felt cold and had a headache; her muscles were tight, and she felt nauseated. She may have said she was coming down with the flu, but she *knew* it was stress.

Sandra couldn't talk to her parents or her friends. Most of her friends, including her on-again-off-again boyfriend, did not phone all week because they were studying too. She was sure that she had not done well on her exams, which might hurt her chances of going to college. Now she wasn't so sure she even wanted to go to college. What was she going to do with the rest of her life?

Sandra was sad, angry and frustrated. She wanted to throw something, break something, or just run away. Two months before, she would have done those things, destroying property and hurting others or herself. Tonight Sandra did not do anything destructive. Instead, she picked up the phone and called Kurt, the counselor from the social services center who had been helping her for the last few months.

When Kurt got the call from Sandra, he knew it had taken courage for her to phone. Her phone call meant she needed help in controlling her reactions to her stressful feelings. After talking for a while, Kurt was able to convey the message to Sandra that she could handle her feelings. Kurt knew that, with his help, Sandra was learning a constructive way of managing her stress. She could make the right decisions now, and she could overcome the wrong choices and actions she had followed in the past.

Kurt is one of the many professional people who can help teenagers cope with stress and manage their emotional and physical reactions to stress. These professionals —including physicians, nurses, clergy, counselors, social workers, and therapists—have special knowledge to help you solve specific problems. They work with individuals, groups, families, children, adolescents, and adults.

Therapists

You may be reluctant to see a counselor or a therapist about stress-related problems. Often teens have a negative view of most counselors, teachers, and school officials. Like most teens, you may just try to cope on your own. However, keeping your feelings to yourself can increase stress and emotional problems. It is important for you to share feelings with others, whether they are friends, family or professional counselors.

"I was so stressed by my parents' divorce, I was ready to try getting stoned to feel better," says Zack, fourteen. "The school counselor could tell things were getting out of control, so she referred me to a therapist. Wait, I thought, I'm not crazy, even if I'm acting a little strange. I found out that a therapist can help normal people who have problems they can't work out by themselves. The therapist helped me to understand my problems and myself. She helped my mom, too, because she was stressed out after the divorce."

A therapist or other counselor can help you learn the skills you need to cope with stress: setting goals, problem solving, anger management, dealing with conflict, and handling change. You can examine the conflicts in your life, build self-esteem, and learn stress management. In family therapy, you can learn to share feelings and learn to communicate. With the help of a therapist, the whole family can learn coping skills.

Sometimes you can help yourself just by talking to friends or family, starting an exercise program, or working on a hobby. How do you know when you should look for professional help? Therapist Greg Newman suggests that whenever you think you might need professional help, that is the time to get it. Be aware of the symptoms of stress but "don't wait for some special signal," Newman says. When your parents see signs of stress, they should speak with your teachers or school counselors.

After a death, a divorce, or other crisis or disaster, it takes a long time to return to what you would consider normal feelings and a normal life. If you think you are hanging onto anger, fear, or other feelings for too long, it is time to seek professional help. You should give yourself time to solve your problem on your own, but set a deadline. If the situation doesn't improve by the deadline, get in touch with a counselor. You probably will be able to sense when your parents are too caught up in their own problems to really focus on your stress and give you the help you need. Counseling can be helpful when your family members are busy with their own concerns.

If you occasionally experience a few symptoms of stress that are not too serious, it is probably just a normal response to everyday problems. However, if you, your parents, or your teacher are aware of many symptoms, occurring often or to a serious degree, it is important to get professional help. Consider seeing a physician first to find the source of the physical problem, whether it seems to be stress-related or not. Don't make your own diagnosis.

It is normal to be sad, anxious, or overwhelmed once in a while, but continuous, severe, or debilitating sadness or anxiety that keeps you from living a normal life may be a sign of depression. You and your parents should be aware of these signs. When they occur, it's important to get medical help without delay.

If stress is causing you to consider some extreme solution to your problem, such as turning to drugs or alcohol, running away, or even attempting suicide, a crisis hotline can provide emergency help. "We don't want anyone to get hurt or to hurt themselves. That is where the crisis hotline really helps," says Greg Newman.

Many hospitals provide outpatient counseling, even in an emergency. As an outpatient, you do not check into the hospital as a patient. Sometimes, teens using alcohol or drugs are brought in by their parents or police. "A teen may walk in feeling suicidal, and we can give him or her immediate attention," one social worker says. Most cities have crisis lines where people may call trained counselors for immediate counseling.

Finding a Counselor

To find a counselor or therapist, start with your school counselor. Many schools provide the service of counselors free to students. Be sure to inform the school—your teacher, principal or counselor—when there is a crisis at home, such as the serious illness or death of a family member, a divorce, or a parent losing a job.

Your school may provide health services that encourage good health practices and reduce stress by answering questions on contraception, sexually transmitted diseases, date rape prevention, and suicide prevention. Your school may be working to prevent or reduce stress among students by teaching conflict resolution and violence prevention. Find out what free services you can get at school or in the community.

If your school counselor thinks you need more help than he or she can provide, he or she may refer you to outside sources—a social worker, psychologist, or a psychiatrist—for further counseling. You can also get a referral from a friend, or your doctor, a member of the clergy, or your local hospital or mental health center. You should like your counselor and feel comfortable working with him or her; otherwise, switch to someone else. A good counselor can help you as an individual and may also help your family learn to communicate and work together.

A social worker who counsels teens with drug or alcohol-related problems suggests that parents need to get into counseling too. When parent and teenager can't talk together, they can start their counseling separately. The aim is that eventually they will come together for counseling and communication.

Many counselors and therapists use a mind-body approach to deal with a patient's stress problems. They give equal attention to a person's mind, body and spirit. Because stress affects you emotionally and physically, you may find this an effective approach.

Most therapists will concentrate on one problem area at a time, starting with the situations that require the most problem solving. The goal is to reinforce appropriate behavior and minimize inappropriate behavior.

Other Resources for Help

Besides school counselors and private-practice therapists, there are many resources in the community that can offer you professional help. There are crisis hotlines in every city that you can phone anonymously for information and advice. A local mental health or social service center may offer outpatient programs for drug addiction or eating disorders. Police often employ social workers or youth workers to counsel teens who may have been locked out of their homes, who are running away, or who are involved with police-related problems.

Responding to a Crisis

Following a crisis or disaster, you may feel like things will never be normal again. You may even think that it is not right to try to get back to a normal situation. However, a counselor who works with disaster victims recommends going back to your normal routine as soon as possible. Be good to yourself. Eat right and get exercise.

You should talk to a counselor soon after the crisis or disaster—away from parents and brothers and sisters, if possible—to discuss your feelings. The longer you wait to talk to a counselor, the more difficult it may be. You don't want to put a shell around yourself, hold in your feelings, or brush problems aside by saying, "Everything is okay." This will only increase your stress.

Try to return to regular activities with friends. This is especially important after your family experiences a crisis such as a fire, when community institutions such as schools, churches and community centers are still intact and ready to help. Getting back to regular activities can also take place after a large-scale disaster, such as a hurricane, but it does take longer because the whole community may be struggling to return to normalcy.

Turning to your Community

Whether your stress is related to a disaster, or comes from the pressures of everyday life, many organizations and support groups in the community can help you directly or indirectly with those problems. Religious organizations, youth groups, civic groups, and scouts may have a support group or social worker to help with stressful situations or may offer activities to help you release stress. You can join or form neighborhood groups that provide mediation programs to help settle conflicts without aggression.

Helping Yourself by Helping Others

Sixteen-year-old Lars likes to talk about some of the activities offered at his community center. "They have a volunteer bureau, so kids who are bored can become volunteers," Lars says. "This was great for me. Last year, school seemed pointless. I started hanging out with some of the kids who were on drugs, my grades were slipping, and I was thinking about dropping out. Deep down my behavior was bothering me, because I had this constant headache and stomachache. I never slept well at all.

"The social worker at the community center recommended that I become a volunteer tutor for little kids who come into the center after school. You would think that adding a job like that might cause even more stress for me, but it didn't. Helping those kids made me feel much better about myself. It also forced me to be a lot more organized. Now I get my own homework done, and my grades are better. I also don't get those headaches and stomachaches anymore. I sleep like a rock, especially on days when I tutor. I hope I can get a job helping out with the community day camp next summer, because then you get paid."

When you care for others, not just when others care for you, it can help you resist stress. Teens who volunteer are often able to build self-esteem and build a feeling of a community, two factors that help reduce stress.

The same is true following a disaster such as a flood or hurricane. You can join the many volunteers at churches, schools, youth groups, and sports clubs who work together at this time of crisis. You can be a part of the network. You can keep busy at a shelter, caring for younger or older people, or you can do physical work such as filling sandbags.

Community Resources

Your local police may have programs that deal with the causes or the results of stress. Stealing, using drugs and alcohol, running away, vandalism, and violent behavior can be the causes of stress or responses to stress. If you are involved in any of these activities, you will probably be involved with the police, and the police may refer you to a counselor.

Work together with your parents, neighbors, and the police to reduce crime and violence, which are major sources of stress. Begin in your own home by turning off violent television shows. Join a neighborhood watch group or form one of your own to work with the police in eliminating drug houses and other criminal elements in your neighborhood.

Hospitals and Health Clinics

If your parent or sibling is hospitalized for a serious illness, you can often find help for your stress right in the hospital. Most hospitals have social workers who can help families deal with stressful problems. Hospital social workers can assist with both the emotional issues and the practical problems of managing a household before and after a patient returns home.

When worries about pregnancy, birth control, and safe sex are causing stress, you can find help in a community health clinic, just as sixteen-year-old Sharone did.

Sharone was so worried about getting pregnant or getting AIDS and other sexually transmitted diseases that it was causing her stress.

Sometimes she had severe headaches. This made Sharone worry even more; did her symptoms mean she really *was* sick or pregnant? Sharone was afraid to talk to her parents about her problems; she was sure they would not understand. They didn't approve of sex before marriage.

Sharone talked to her friend, Mei, who suggested that Sharone go to a local health clinic set up especially for young women. "For a small fee, you can get an exam, and they will test for infections and diseases," Mei explained. "It's confidential. They won't tell your parents or anyone else."

It took a while for Sharone to get up the courage to make an appointment at the clinic. The first time she went, she was part of a small chat group that discussed pregnancy, birth control, and sexually transmitted diseases. Just talking to the other girls and discovering that they had similar worries made Sharone feel better. Finding out after her pelvic exam that she had no physical problems also reduced Sharone's stress symptoms.

Sharone now knew that she could always go to the clinic to discuss problems with the counselor. Sharone paid for the clinical visits with money she earned at her after-school job. This gave her a feeling of responsibility and control of her own life, something that also helped to reduce her stress. "It's not easy, but it's something I'm doing for myself," Sharone told Mei.

Many hospitals offer inpatient and outpatient programs

for teens with behavioral or mental health problems that cause stress or that are the result of stress. Often a special program or individual, family, or group therapy is supervised by a team of professionals that includes medical doctors, psychologists, therapists, teachers, and social workers. Inpatient programs may be followed by outpatient counseling after school.

Religious Organizations

Religious institutions often provide a variety of programs, such as support groups and counseling, that can help teens reduce the stress in their lives. Religious observance itself may help reduce stress. Some therapists, even those not directly connected with a religious institution, incorporate a spiritual side to counseling. "It helps us to explain and live with our problems," one therapist says.

Stress Management Programs

You may need a special stress management program when your family or home situation is the source of your stress. If your family has experienced divorce, abuse, the illness or death of a family member, if your parent is having a problem dealing with his or her own stress, or if you live in a dangerous area, you may want to find a program that will provide support and help to relieve the stress you feel.

A group such as Big Brothers and Big Sisters may be able to help. Called a "mentor program," Big Brothers and Big Sisters gives teenagers positive role models. In this program, adult volunteers take the place of a parent or friend. They are role models because many of them grew up under the same conditions as many of the teens in the group and are now successful. A teen has someone to talk to who will listen to problems and concerns and provide advice and support. Being involved in this program can help build self-esteem.

A teen may also gain new experiences through these groups. Teens can learn that there are more options in life than what they see—more beyond their own dreams, friends, and home. They can get away from peer pressure, gangs, drugs, and the isolation of their own neighborhood.

"I am not only graduating from high school this year, but I am going to college this fall," says seventeen-year-old Aidan. "I've got to give a lot of credit to my Big Brother, Steve. He's not really my big brother, but he comes from the Big Brothers organization.

"It's a long story, starting with my dad walking out on us a few years ago. He left me with my mom, three sisters, and my grandmother: all women! I couldn't stand it. I was always angry, ready to tear things apart. I wouldn't go to school and I wouldn't do anything my mom or Gramma wanted me to do. I was this close to joining a gang when I heard about Big Brothers. Before I met Steve, I was afraid he was going to be some goody-two-shoes, but no way. He grew up in my neighborhood, without a father, and now he owns a business.

"We would get together on Saturdays and do things like shoot baskets. Steve always made me finish my home-work first. Usually Gramma took my sisters with her to do the laundry, and my mother was working, so the apart-ment was quiet. Steve convinced me to go to school and to stay in school. My teachers and the school counselor couldn't believe the change in me, but I think it's because Steve helped me feel good about myself, and he helped me cope with a lot of stress. If he could succeed, then I could succeed."

You can relate one-on-one with a mentor, as Aidan did, to address your problems. You can also benefit from working with a group.

Support Groups

Support groups can help you cope with stress. In a support group, several people with similar problems get together with or without a counselor for discussion and support. Support groups cover a wide variety of subjects. You can find an appropriate support group whether you need to talk about your parents' divorce, your mom's unemployment, the illness or death (including suicide) of a family member or friend, an eating disorder, or a problem with drugs or alcohol.

In a support group, you can share you feelings and anxieties with people who may feel the same way. When you learn that others are experiencing similar emotions, you know that you are not alone, and you know that you are not abnormal. It can boost your self-esteem and your ability to cope with your situation. People who belong to support groups are often less likely than others to respond negatively to stress.

A support group is a place where you can talk and learn how to handle your problems. It can help reduce stress by encouraging members to face their problems and find the courage to deal with them. Members can learn how others faced similar problems and succeeded in coping with them. Groups also provide social support and comfort for members, which is an important factor in reducing stress. You can share your successes as well as your stresses.

Participation in a support group can even improve physical health. Less stress means lower blood pressure and less muscle tension. People who experience the social support of a group tend to take better care of themselves by eating well, getting more sleep, exercising, and avoiding harmful habits such as smoking and drinking. These measures help reduce the effects of stress, so it becomes a positive cycle.

A support group might be sponsored by a hospital, social service agency, church or synagogue, school, or just an interested group of friends or neighbors. If you find a need for a special support group in your community, try to organize it yourself. You are taking control of a situation and that, in itself, can help reduce stress.

A support group may be the only place where you can share your feelings about serious problems. Even a best friend may be uncomfortable talking to you. That's what happened to Alicia.

"Fiona and I grew up together, and we were always best friends," Alicia says. "When my dad died from heart failure, Fiona seemed to disappear. After the funeral, she came with her parents to our house, but she just stood at the back of the room. When I went back to school, none of the kids seemed to want to talk to me. I felt so isolated. I was so stressed, I couldn't eat or sleep. All I wanted to do was sit on my bed and cry. I was surprised that my friends had abandoned me.

"Luckily Mom signed me up for a bereavement support group at the local hospital. There I could talk to other kids who had lost a parent to heart problems. I also learned how to manage my stress. It takes a long time to get over your grief, even with a support group. They don't give you a timetable and say you should be over your grief by a certain date. The group makes you feel comfortable, and that helps reduce the stress.

"It took a couple of months before the kids at school treated me normally again. Fiona told me she was afraid to talk to me because she didn't know what to say. She was afraid she would say the wrong thing and make me feel even worse. I've got to thank the support group for helping me not feel totally alone."

A pastor or rabbi may lead a support group for those who have a family member who is terminally ill or dying. There are also special support groups for teens who have lost a family member to suicide. In this situation, the whole family will probably need counseling.

Peer Counseling

Recognizing that teens have the power to help other teens, many schools and religious organizations are establishing peer counseling groups. In peer counseling, young people are trained to steer other teens in the right direction.

By teaching problem-solving strategies and other skills, peer counseling gives teenagers the opportunity to solve many of their own conflicts. Peer counseling can be used to resolve conflicts between teens in school.

Peer counselors can also help other teens to deal with personal problems.

Sixteen-year-old Glenn discovered his school's peer counseling group when he had some stressful problems at home. "I couldn't talk to my parents, because I thought they were the cause of all my problems in the first place," Glenn says. "I was ready to do something desperate, like running away. Then I started working with the peer counseling group. In a group like that you learn how other people handled similar problems. You also find out that you can cope, because they did. Your problem won't last forever if you deal with it the right way. You need to talk, and you need someone to listen. At the same time, you listen to someone else, so you help each other."

Whatever the stressful situation in your life, there are resources you can turn to for help. These organizations are there to help you begin to realize that you can cope with your problems, even if it takes a long time before they no longer cause you stress. It is important for you to remember that you do not have to handle your problems alone. Feeling alone can be very stressful in itself.

How Not to Cope with Stress

"I'm sure that a lot of the teens who get into trouble with the law are really acting out as a way of coping with stress," says Ross, a social worker for a police department. "Today's teens have to put up with a lot of stress, a lot more than I ever did. There are problems at home, problems in school and out on the street, and worries about drugs and pregnancy. Even though they are educated about the risks of their behavior, kids still do things that get them into trouble. That's what frightens me. Kids are out stealing, setting fires, using drugs and alcohol. If their behavior is related to stress, then they are choosing coping mechanisms that are unhealthy."

When you are under stress, you want to cope with it in positive ways that reduce the stress. Often teens—and adults, too—deal with their stress in ways they think will reduce it, but these may actually increase stress. You may try to mask your stress by rationalizing that it isn't so bad or that you don't need help; by denying that you are under stress; by acting out with violent, aggressive behavior; or by turning to drugs, alcohol or tobacco. These are the wrong actions to take. They can lead to more serious physical and emotional problems.

There are many activities that may seem to decrease stress for a brief period. Activities such as drinking beverages containing alcohol or caffeine, smoking, taking drugs, watching a lot of television, daydreaming, or simply ignoring the problem are "quick fix" solutions that do not solve anything. These actions not only do not reduce stress, but they are also likely to increase your stress. You must stop the cycle and find more productive ways to decrease the amount of stress you feel.

When Magdalena first began high school, the number of essays she suddenly had to write completely overwhelmed her. "Writing papers always takes me forever," she says. "I have a lot of trouble organizing what I want to say. I would finish one assignment and then be so burnt out that I would need to take a breather before beginning the next one. By that time, I was usually right up against the deadline. I'd be up all night the night before the due date, trying to finish. I'd get so nervous that I wouldn't be able to concentrate. I started sneaking some of my mom's diet pills. I knew that they would give me energy.

"They gave me energy all right, but they also made me jittery. And after the effects wore off, I would crash. Sometimes, I could barely stay awake in class. When midterm exams came, my life became a nightmare. I took pills so that I could study, but then when I went to write my exams, I was so drowsy I couldn't answer any questions. I failed basically all of my midterms and was ready to have a nervous breakdown. I broke down and had a big long talk with my parents, who encouraged me to meet with my teachers and work out a study plan for each of my courses. My English teacher, Mr. Robitaille, said that there were lots of students with problems similar to mine. He told me that many of them had done much better after they had begun participating in his writing lab. I began attending the lab. Not only did my paper-writing skills improve, but I found it eased my stress to talk to the other students in the group. As for the pills, I'm never going near them again."

Rationalizing Stress

Everyone experiences stress to some degree. Denying that you have stress, and therefore not dealing with it, is not a healthy response to your stress. First you need to recognize that there is a problem. Then you can start to deal with the problem and start making changes. When you put off your problem, hoping it will just go away by itself, you are actually wasting the energy you need to respond to your stress in a positive way.

Because they want to avoid the stress a disaster might cause, some people may deny the possibility of a disaster, especially a natural disaster. They ignore warnings and do not even take simple precautions. However, preparing for a disaster or doing something to reduce the risk of disaster gives you a sense of control that can help to reduce stress.

Artificial Stress Reducers

Turning to alcohol, tobacco, or drugs is not the way to cope with stress. These substances may be popular remedies for stress, but they offer only temporary relief. Alcohol may make you feel relaxed and happy when you first try it. However, the more you drink, the less relaxed and happy you feel. Drinking can lead to a variety of physical and emotional problems, including liver and heart disease, anxiety, depression, and disturbed sleep.

Drugs and alcohol can be habit-forming. They create more problems and may only compound the stress you are feeling. When you are under the influence of drugs or alcohol, you reduce your ability to control the sources of stress in your life. Control is an important factor in coping with stress.

In the short term, smoking may seem to reduce stress by making you feel more relaxed. Smoking may make you feel more alert and less anxious. In the long term, however, smoking causes a variety of physical problems that increase stress and the symptoms of stress, such as high blood pressure, heart disease, and breathing problems. Smoking may impair blood circulation and breathing and can cause sleep disorders. It can also reduce your immunity to infectious diseases and may lead to stroke, heart disease, and cancer.

Prescribed medications and over-the-counter drugs, such as sleeping pills and tranquilizers, may help you to feel relaxed and can reduce the symptoms of stress. However, tranquilizers may make you drug dependent and can be very dangerous when taken in large doses or with alcohol or other drugs. They also can impair the way you feel and act during the day. They can make you feel tired or depressed.

The use of alcohol, tobacco, or drugs in an attempt to cope with stress only covers up the symptoms of stress and does not deal with the source of stress. You need to go beyond just treating the symptoms in order to be able to actually come to terms with the problem.

"I was so nervous about auditioning for the piano concerto competition, I was a real wreck," says sixteen-year-old Renata. "Everything seemed to hurt: my head, my stomach, my muscles. I was stressed out. So, I took a tranquilizer that my doctor had prescribed. I also took some aspirin. It didn't work the way I had hoped. When I got to the audition, I was relaxed, but I also couldn't play well. I couldn't concentrate on the music, and I kept making mistakes. Of course I didn't win the competition. As it turned out, the medication only made me feel depressed; and after it wore off, I had the biggest headache ever."

The Effects of Food and Drink

What you eat and drink—and the way you eat and drink—may seem to reduce stress, but poor eating and drinking habits can affect you emotionally as well as physically. For instance, caffeine, found in coffee and many colas, may at first create a feeling of alertness and better concentration. But these feelings are soon reduced, causing you to "crash" and feel sluggish later on. Too much caffeine can cause stomach disorders, irregular heartbeat, and headaches.

Candy and other foods containing sugar can give you a feeling of energy, but this is quickly followed by a letdown that leaves you feeling irritable and tired. Chocolate also contains caffeine. Sugary foods may also cause tooth decay and weight gain, two problems that can add to your stress. A balanced diet combined with exercise will keep your energy level steady and will help you maintain a healthy body weight.

Eating Disorders

Food is essential for living. For most people, eating can also be an enjoyable social event. However, there are people who turn to food—or turn away from food—to reduce their feelings of stress. Some may develop an eating disorder such as anorexia nervosa or bulimia. Others will overeat and gain a large amount of weight. Eating disorders are symptoms of stress. Improper eating habits will not reduce stress. They can only increase stress and may lead to serious health problems.

"I don't know what happened to my friend Alison," says Leah, sixteen. "Things seemed to be going so well for her. She was one of the best students in the class. She had the lead in the school play, and she was homecoming princess for the big football game. But then she stopped eating and she started to lose a lot of weight. When I asked her what was wrong, the only thing she said was, 'It's hard for me to do everything that's expected of me.' Alison got so thin, she had to drop out of school at the end of her sophomore year and go into the hospital. Mom told me that Alison had anorexia.

"Alison is back at school now, and she looks a little better. She told me that she has learned to manage her stress better. I didn't know that stress, or at least coping with stress in the wrong way, could affect you like that."

If you suspect that you or someone you know has an

eating disorder, it is vital to seek medical help right away. Eating disorders can result in death if they are left untreated for too long a period of time.

Problems in Relationships

Close relationships with family and friends are important. By giving you the opportunity to talk and to share feelings with people who care about you, these relationships can help you avoid stress as well as cope with stress. However, in an effort to deal with their stress, some teens find themselves involved in a harmful relationship. When you find your values differ greatly or your opinions conflict with a friend or relative, the relationship can be more stressful than helpful. Relationships that include physical or emotional abuse can only increase stress and may lead to serious physical or emotional damage.

"Acting Out"

Jane Gaitskill, a social worker who counsels teens, says that teens often react to stress by acting out, and getting into trouble at home or at school. They may refuse to do their homework and may turn to drugs. "This behavior will never reduce stress, and probably will increase it," Gaitskill says.

Venting your anger may sometimes make you feel better, but in reality it is not the proper way to deal with stress. When you curse, threaten, intimidate, or try to exert excessive control by demanding your way and being the center of attention, you are not taking action to reduce your stress.

Violent and Reckless Behavior

Violent behavior is always unacceptable. If your stress makes you feel like lashing out, turn instead to physical exercise or work. David lifts weights when he feels angry. "All that energy I might waste on anger goes into my lifts and helps to improve them," he says.

"I like my after-school ceramics class for that reason," says Glenda, fourteen. "When I get angry, I feel like throwing things. In ceramics class, I can really throw that clay on the wheel and pound it. Instead of breaking things, I come out with something creative."

When a teen has survived a disaster but is not coping well in the aftermath, he or she might adopt the attitude that "nothing can hurt me now." He or she may turn to inappropriate behavior and try risky activities, such as drugs or reckless driving.

Expressing anger by acting out violently cannot reduce stress. On the other hand, holding in feelings can lead to serious physical and emotional stress symptoms. That is why it is important to communicate your feelings in an appropriate manner. Both repressing feelings and acting out are the wrong ways to cope.

Negative Thinking

You are thinking negatively when you dwell on the bad side of an issue, exaggerating the negative and minimizing the positive. Negative thinking will not reduce your stress, but can only add to it. Negative thoughts can lead to inappropriate feelings, which in turn lead to unacceptable behavior.

Negative thinking may include the following:

- **Worrying about stressful situations without taking some action to solve them:** Some people even worry about situations that don't yet exist.
- **Deciding that you have to solve your problems by yourself:** "No one else can help me with this problem."
- **Trying to handle all your problems at once:** If you believe that you must deal with and eliminate all your problems at once rather than working on one problem at a time over a long period of time, you may not succeed in eliminating any problem.
- **Overgeneralizing:** "I'm always wrong," "Nobody likes me," "If I can't solve this problem, I can't solve any problems."
- **Jumping to conclusions:** "I know they won't like my speech in English class."

Many of these negative thoughts can become self-fulfilling prophesies, meaning that thinking about them will make them come true. You may not prepare your speech well enough because "nobody will like it anyway." Fearing rejection at a party or when starting a new school, you may not try to be friendly to others, and they will reject you because they think you are unfriendly.

Negative thinking occurs when you worry not only about a situation but also about the stress the situation will cause you. That worry can be even more stressful than the situation itself.

This happened to fifteen-year-old Mia. She arranged a trip to the theater for her church's youth group. She sent out publicity, took reservations, bought the tickets, and arranged for transportation. At the same time, Mia worried whether her friends would like the play.

"I was under too much stress," Mia says. "Here I was doing all this work, which was stressful to begin with. Instead of giving myself credit for doing a good job, I worried whether people would like the play, which only added to my stress. It was giving me headaches and stomachaches. In fact, on the night of the play, I had a hard time enjoying the show. I think that if I had emphasized the positive instead of the negative, I would have had a lot less stress, and I would have enjoyed the evening a lot more. After all my worrying, everyone loved the play, and a lot of people thanked me for making the arrangements. I wished I could have been more confident from the beginning."

Think about how you usually respond to stressful situations. If you react with negative thinking or denial, or if you react by getting angry, resorting to violence, taking drugs, smoking, drinking, or eating badly, you are adding stress, not reducing it. Social worker Jim Gorski advises teens to act upon their stress, not just react to it. Do something positive to bring about a change that will reduce or eliminate the stressor, or make a change in your response to that stressor.

Avoiding Stress (Sometimes)

"I think writing this term paper has been a real education, and not just because I learned a lot about the subject of the paper," says sixteen-year-old Rashid. "I was really stressed out over this paper. I started it too late, and I had to rush at the end. I skipped meals to work on it, and I couldn't sleep at night worrying about it. That only made it harder to write the paper the next day. It gave me a giant-sized headache."

"I finished the paper and handed it in on time. But I've learned my lesson. Now I know that I could have avoided a lot of stress if I had started earlier and was more organized. I should have eaten right and gotten more sleep, and even done some exercising and relaxing. That would have done it: good-bye, stress!"

Stress Is Part of Life

Everyone experiences stress from time to time to some degree. It's not possible to avoid all stressful situations. You would not want to avoid all stress, anyway. In some instances, a little stress is good: It may help you perform better on the basketball court or push you to study longer for an exam. We will discuss the positive side of stress later in this chapter.

There are things you can do to avoid some stress, such as establishing good eating and sleeping patterns, getting organized and planning ahead, and communicating with family and friends.

There are many good reasons to make wise lifestyle choices. Eating right, getting enough sleep, and exercising (all those things your parents, teachers, and doctors tell you to do) will help keep you physically healthy. These are also just the kinds of things that can help you to avoid stress, reduce stress, and cope with stress. If you are in good physical shape when you experience stress, your stress may have less negative effects on your body.

Establish good eating habits. Good eating habits include having a good breakfast every day. A good meal to start the day raises your energy level, so you are better prepared to face the stressors that may await you. During the day, eat regular meals that include fruits, vegetables, protein, and whole grains. Cut down on fats, salt, and sugar.

Avoid caffeine and alcohol. Eating or drinking products with caffeine, including chocolate, cola, and coffee, can make you feel stressed even when there is no reason for the stress. Caffeine can interfere with a restful sleep. Alcohol is a depressant, which means that even if at first it makes you feel better, it will eventually impair your ability to cope with stress.

Get enough sleep. When you are overtired, a problem may seem much bigger than it actually is. Try to maintain a regular sleep schedule, and get up about the same time every day, even on the weekends. This kind of routine is less stressful than not getting enough sleep during the week and then trying to catch up on the weekends.

Learn relaxation techniques. To reduce stress, use relaxation techniques, such as deep breathing, especially before a stressful event like giving a speech or taking a test. Regular **exercise** not only makes you feel better and look better, but it can also modify the way your body responds to stress. Your body can recover more quickly from the physical effects of stress if it is in good physical condition.

Learn problem-solving techniques. When you are under stress, or before a situation causes you stress, take time to understand the real problem and the best way to approach it. Consider more than one option.

Get organized. If you organize your activities and manage your time effectively, you will not only avoid a lot of stress, but you will also discover many other benefits. You are probably a busy person with many activities, including classes, homework, sports, music lessons, or other after-school activities, such as a part-time job. You may have a variety of responsibilities at home, including baby-sitting, cleaning, and helping out with meals. When you have many activities, you can become overwhelmed, which can cause stress. If you try to do everything at once, you may actually accomplish very little, and that can cause even more stress.

It's a good idea to keep a calendar, not only to write down school assignments but for other dates and appointments, too. Leila has two calendars, one just for her social life, the other one for school. "I can't live without either one," Leila says. "The first things I buy when school starts are my assignment notebooks."

Set priorities. Instead of trying to do all your activities

135

in too little time, pace yourself and do one task at a time. List your activities in order of importance, and do the most important ones first. If you have a task that can be completed quickly, you might do that one first to give yourself a morale boost. If one task is overwhelming by itself, try to break it up into parts; for instance, you may not be able to wash all of the windows in your apartment in one day, but you may be able to wash all of the front windows and get the back ones done in a day or two.

If you need assistance with a difficult project, don't hesitate to **ask for help.** You will not only find your work easier, which helps reduce stress, but you will enjoy the support of another person.

Leave some unscheduled time in your work for interruptions or emergencies, as well as time for relaxation or exercise; remember, they are stress fighters. Don't forget to **mix in some fun** activities with your more serious obligations.

It's stressful when you don't have enough time to accomplish what you need to do and what you want to do. Good **time management** can help to prevent that stress. First, **set goals.** Make a list of things you have to do and things you want to do. Be realistic. Include short-term goals for the next few days and weeks. Don't forget a plan for long-term goals as well. For instance, if one of your goals is making the varsity track team, you have to include in your time schedule the practice and training it will take to reach that goal.

Keep everything in perspective. When setting goals, be realistic. Goals should be neither too high, so that they are unreachable, nor too low, so they offer no incentive.

Accept that you can't do everything. **Have a sense of humor and optimism.**

Try to **maintain a balance** between extremes in your life. Find the "happy medium" between trying to accomplish everything by yourself and only depending on the support and assistance of others. Maintain a balance between what you ought to do and what you want to do. Be aware of what you can control and know that you can't have control over every situation.

Get involved in activities at school; in your church, synagogue, or mosque; or in the community. Volunteer work can boost your feelings of self-esteem.

If you work part-time or full-time, try to **do something that you enjoy** so you care enough to do a good job. If you don't care for the work, try at least to pick one part of it that you do like. If you get no satisfaction at all from your work, you will only add to your stress.

"I guess I'm lucky I got this job as a receptionist for a manufacturer," says April, seventeen. "The pay is pretty good, but the work is sort of boring. I actually started to feel nervous because I wasn't doing enough work. But then I noticed that the display case in the reception area was just sitting there empty. I asked my boss if I could put in some kind of display, and he said okay.

"Planning what to put in the display case uses my creativity. Working on it fills in the time when I don't have anything else to do. Now work is much more interesting for me, and I look forward to coming to work. I don't have those stressful feelings anymore, either."

Stay in control of yourself and your life as much as possible. Not all stressors can be avoided. Others are completely under your control. For instance, an unplanned pregnancy can be a major source of stress, but it can be prevented. Become informed about pregnancy, birth control, and sexually transmitted diseases, and act positively from that knowledge.

For the stressors that can't be avoided, a **positive attitude** can make a difference in how much stress you feel. For example, change can be stressful, but viewing change as a challenge or a new experience can reduce the stress. Try to be open to new experiences.

When you are in control of a situation, it gives you the confidence that you can manage the situation and even turn events to your advantage; you then feel less stressed. The less control you have over a situation, the more stressful it is.

Jakub, fifteen, learned first-hand about control and stress. "I have a part-time job in a take-out delicatessen. During the week, I work the counter by myself. Sometimes it gets pretty hectic, but I've established my own routine that allows me to serve customers quickly and efficiently. Clients are always happy and my boss knows I do a good job.

"The problem is on weekends. It gets so busy that my boss hired another counter person, Byron. At first Byron was slow, and he made mistakes. I'd get stressed when it got crowded because I'd feel responsible not only for doing my job, but his as well. But one day, it was so busy that I didn't have time to watch Byron. He screwed up a big order, and I didn't catch it. The customer complained to my boss, and my boss really let me have it. He said that since I had been there the longest, I should have been in control of the situation. I was so frustrated I felt like quitting. Luckily, I cooled off and then had a talk with Byron. Instead of trying to do his job for him, we worked out that he would come in before his shift so I could teach him my routine. That way, I had control over the situation and less stress."

Control also means you need to **think for yourself** and not give in to peer pressure. Samuel Huff, a counselor in a midwestern inner-city school, advises his students to be independent. "Don't just go along with the crowd. Think for yourself; use your own good mind. You know right from wrong; so don't go along when you know something is wrong," Huff says. "This is a sign of emotional and moral maturity."

As you mature, you need to **take responsibility for your actions.** Taking responsibility puts you in control, and control helps you avoid or reduce stress. To make it easier, try role playing. You can rehearse what you want to say and how you want to act in order to resist peer pressure to smoke, drink, or take drugs. A lot of people (adults and other teens) may be ready to tell you what you should do. However, this is your opportunity to think for yourself and take control.

Don't fear stress, but do anticipate it. If you **anticipate stress,** you may be able to avoid it or reduce it. However, there are two sides to anticipating stress. On the positive side, when you feel that a situation may cause you stress, you can take time out, assess the situation, and decide on a response. "Rehearse" stressful situations. This way you can gain some sense of control. You may not be able to control every situation, but you can plan your response and reduce the stress that an event may cause. The negative side of anticipation occurs when you only worry that a situation will cause you stress. That worry can be even more stressful than the circumstance itself.

To calm down when anticipating stress, ask yourself: "What is the worst thing that can happen?" Then consider how likely it is that the worst will occur. Plan in advance what you will do if it does happen. This will help you feel more prepared for any outcome.

Being independent and in control does not mean that you should avoid contact with other people. On the contrary, many social workers and psychologists agree that having **close relationships** with family, friends, and other people in the community is one of the best ways to avoid stress or to cope with stress. Seek out at least one adult whom you trust and who cares about you, such as a parent, an aunt or uncle, a teacher, counselor, coach, member of the clergy, neighbor, or employer. Close relationships with relatives and friends help you to avoid some stress and reduce the symptoms of stress. However, it is important that you belong to a peer group that shares your values.

The Good Side of Stress

Everyone experiences stress to some degree in their everyday lives. Stress cannot be totally eliminated from your life. You probably wouldn't want to avoid all stress, anyway. That would mean that your life was pretty dull. Remember, some stress comes from happy events, such as graduation or going on vacation. A moderate amount of stress can give us more energy and motivation to succeed.

Beyond keeping life interesting and exciting, stress has several other benefits.

Stress can be a warning sign of other problems in our lives. It tells us that something needs to be recognized and acted upon. You can learn from stress. "I started getting tight muscles whenever I went to gymnastics practice. I couldn't perform at my best; it was almost like an injury," says Janie, fifteen. "My coach said it was stress, probably because I had too many other activities. I was trying to get top grades in school, too. My 'injury' made me look at my life. I needed to get organized, and I needed to decide if I really should be doing all the activities I was involved in.

"Well, I did get organized, and I did drop a couple of activities that I was doing only because someone else thought I should do them. Now I don't have the tight muscles, and I'm performing better in gymnastics. I even have more time for studying. I guess you could say that stress helped me because it forced me to make changes that improved my life."

When you rehearse or prepare for a potential situation that may be stressful, such as a natural disaster, you are also educating yourself. Learning about disaster preparedness may not only reduce the stress you feel before and after the disaster occurs, but may also provide knowledge that will help you cope with day-to-day problems. The fight-or-flight reaction that takes over after a disaster can help you to help yourself and others.

Preparing for a disaster or doing something to reduce the risk of disaster gives you some control over the situation and can help reduce stress. When you survive disasters, you gain new feelings of confidence and of self-esteem;

you have mastered a tremendous challenge.

A moderate amount of stress can help improve athletic performance. You need some stress or stimulation to do your best. A little stress can be useful, increasing your performance and efficiency. However, a lot of stress or continuous stress can lead to a bad performance.

Change can be stressful, but it can also be viewed as an opportunity. Change may help you improve the quality of your life by giving you new choices. When you deal with stress, you have an opportunity to reevaluate your life, to set new goals and priorities, and to improve relationships. Stress can be beneficial, but only in a moderate amount, and only when you try to cope with it. You cannot eliminate all stress, but you can deal with it in many ways, and that is how you can improve your life.

You can look at stress and your efforts to cope with stress as a challenge and an opportunity. Successfully coping with stress can improve your self-esteem and competence. When you deal with your stress, you grow as a person. By using problem-solving skills and finding alternatives to stressful situations, you may find your life going in a new direction.

Glossary

anorexia nervosa An eating disorder characterized by dramatic weight loss, compulsive dieting, lack of appetite, and fear of gaining weight.

anti-semitic Showing prejudice against people of Jewish descent.

biofeedback A technique for monitoring and modifying the body's response to stress.

bulimia An eating disorder in which eating binges are followed by strict dieting, strenuous exercise, vomiting and/or the use of laxatives in order to purge food.

compulsive disorder A physiological condition in which a person performs certain actions repeatedly for no apparent reason.

crisis A situation of extreme change, with either a positive or negative impact.

fight-or-flight response The natural human impulse to defend oneself or flee when confronted with a threatening situation.

immunity The body's ability to fight off or protect against disease.

phobia A strong fear, usually irrational and excessive, of a particular thing or situation.

positive thinking A confident, self-assured way of looking at oneself and the world.

post-traumatic stress disorder An extreme stress response, arising from a disaster or crisis, in which a person relives the trauma and continues to be emotionally tied up in it.

prejudice The expression of bias or intolerance against another person without reason.

racism The belief that a race of people is superior to others.

restricted environment stimulus therapy (R.E.S.T.) A method of reducing stress by minimizing all external stimuli.

sexually transmitted disease Any disease that is transmitted from person to person through sexual contact.

stressor A condition, situation, or incident that causes stress.

type A personality A person who is usually tense, aggressive, and driven to perform or succeed.

Where to Go for Help

Listed below are a few of the many organizations that can help you with your stress or with a specific source of stress. You can also find information at the public library, community center, mental health association, or hospital. Your telephone directory also lists organizations and resources for help in your area.

In the United States

Alateen
P.O. Box 862
Midtown Station
New York, NY 10018
(212) 302-7240

American Institute of Stress
124 Park Avenue
Yonkers, NY 10703
(914) 963-1200
e-mail: stress124@earthlink.net
Web site: http://www.stress.org/

American Red Cross/Disaster Mental Health Program
Mid-America Chapter
43 East Ohio Street
Chicago, IL 60611
(312) 440-2140

American Self-Help Clearing House
St. Clares Hospital
25 Pocono Road
Denville, NJ 07834
(973) 625-9565
e-mail: ashc@cybernex. net
Web site: http://www.cmhc.com/selfhelp

Anxiety Disorders Association of America
11900 Parklawn Drive, Suite 100
Rockville, MD 20852
(301) 231-9350
e-mail: anxdis@adaa.com
Web site: http://www.adaa.org/

Big Brothers Big Sisters of America
230 North 13th Street
Philadelphia, PA 19107
(215) 567-7000
e-mail: bbbsa@aol.com
Web site: http://www.bbsa.org

Families Anonymous
P.O. Box 3457
Colver City, CA 90231-3457
(800) 736-9805
(310) 313-5800
e-mail: famanon@aol.com

Families with Children
Hospice of the North Shore
2821 Central Street
Evanston, IL 60201
(847) HOSPICE (467-7423)

International Society for Traumatic Stress Studies
60 Revere Drive, Suite 500
Northbrook, IL 60062
(847) 480-9028
e-mail: www@istss.org
Web site: http://www.istss.org

National Anxiety Foundation
3135 Custer Drive
Lexington, KY 40517-4001
(606) 272-7166
http://www.lexington-on-line.com/naf.html

National Association of Anorexia Nervosa and
    Associated Disorders
P.O. Box 7
Highland Park, IL 60035
(847) 831-3438

National Institute of Mental Health
U.S. Department of Health and Human Services
5600 Fishers Lane
Rockville, MD 20857
(301) 443-4513
For information on depression: (800) 421-4211
For information on panic: (800) 64-PANIC (647-2642)
For information on anxiety: (888) ANXIETY (269-4389)
e-mail: nimhinfo@nih.gov
Web site: http://www.nimh.nih.gov

National Mental Health Association
    Information Center
(800) 969-NMHA (6642)

Overeaters Anonymous
6075 Zenith Court NE
Rio Rancho, NM 87124
(505) 981-2664)

Planned Parenthood Federation of America
810 Seventh Avenue
New York, NY 10019
(212) 541-7800)
e-mail: communication@ppfa.org
Web site: http://www.ppfa.org/ppfa

Self Help Center
150 North Wacker Drive
Chicago, IL 60606
(312) 368-9070

In Canada:
Al-Anon/Alateen
1771 Avenue Road
P.O. Box 54533
North York, Ontario M5M 4N5
(416) 410-3809
Web site: http://web.idirect.com/~alanon

Big Brothers and Sisters of Canada
3228 South Service Road
Burlington, Ontario L7N 3H8
1-800-263-9133
e-mail: bbsc@bbsc.ca
Web site: http://www.bbsc.ca/index.html

Canadian Mental Health Association
2160 Yonge Street
Toronto, Ontario M4S 2Z3
(416) 484-7750

Canadian Red Cross Society
1430 Blair Place
Gloucester, Ontario K1J 9N2
(613) 740-1900
e-mail: feedback@redcross.ca
Web site: http://www.redcross.ca/

Canadian Traumatic Stress Network
Contact: Teresa Cryer
3727 Trans-Canada Highway, RR#1
Tappen, British Columbia V0E 2X0
(250) 835-4473
e-mail: ctsn@jetstream.net
Web site: http://play.psych.mun.ca/~dhart/trauma_net/

Planned Parenthood Federation of Canada
1 Nicholas Street, Suite 430
Ottawa, Ontario K1N 7B7
(613) 241-4474

For Further Reading

Beckelman, Laurie. *Stress*. New York: Crestwood House, 1994.

Buckingham, Robert, Ph.D., and Sandra Huggard. *Coping with Grief*. Rev. ed. New York: The Rosen Publishing Group, 1993.

Cush, Cathie. *Depression* (Teen Hotline). Austin, TX: Raintree/Steck Vaughn, 1994.

Feldman, Robert S. *Understanding Stress*. New York: Franklin Watts, 1992.

Gallo, Donald R. *No Easy Answers: Short Stories About Teenagers Making Tough Choices*. New York: Bantam Books, 1997.

Hipp, Earl, and Pamela Espeland. *Fighting Invisible Tigers: A Stress Management Guide for Teens*. Minneapolis, MN: Free Spirit, 1996.

Inlander, Charles B. *Stress: Ways to Relieve Tension and Stay Healthy*. New York: Walker & Co., 1996.

Kubersky, Rachel. *Eating Disorders: Anorexia and Bulimia*. New York: The Rosen Publishing Group, 1999.

McCoy, Kathy, and Charles Wibbelsman. *Life Happens: A Teenager's Guide to Friends, Failure, Sexuality, Love, Rejection, Addiction, Peer Pressure, Families, Loss, Depression, Change, and Other Challenges of Living*. New York: Berkley Publishing Group, 1996.

Newman, Susan. Don't Be S.A.D.: *A Teenage Guide to Handling Stress, Anxiety and Depression*. Englewood Cliffs, NJ: Julian Messner, 1991.

Packard, Gwen K. *Coping When a Parent Goes Back to Work.* New York: The Rosen Publishing Group, 1995.

Porterfield, Kay Marie. *Straight Talk About Post-Traumatic Stress Disorder: Coping with the Aftermath of Trauma. New York:* Facts on File, 1996.

Sherrow, Victoria. *Mental Illness.* San Diego, CA: Lucent Books, 1996.

Silverstein, Alvin, et al. *Depression* (Diseases and People). Springfield, NJ: Enslow Publishers, 1999.

Simpson, Carolyn, and Dwain Simpson. *Coping with Post-Traumatic Stress Disorder.* New York: Rosen Publishing Group, 1997.

Sommers, Annie Leah. *Everything You Need to Know About Looking and Feeling Your Best: A Guide for Girls.* New York: The Rosen Publishing Group, 1999.

Sommers, Michael A. *Everything You Need to Know About Looking and Feeling Your Best: A Guide for Guys.* New York: The Rosen Publishing Group, 1999.

Index